Unchained Child of the Most High God

Unchained Child of the Most High God

Let God free the captive and redeem the conqueror in you.

GILLIAN HERMAN-DAVIS

ISBN-13: 9780692450383
ISBN-10: 0692450386
Library of Congress Control Number: 2015907865
Grace Sufficient Publishing, Jonesboro, GA

In loving memory of my father: Randolph Herman. He taught me to approach life with courage and to never give up.

To my other parents and God-parents, siblings, cousins, uncles and aunts: you inspired this work in many ways.

To my husband, Morris Davis, who gives me strength and teaches me unconditional love.

To my friends, who have become more like brothers and sisters to me.

To Faye Herring and her husband, the late Bob Herring: She showed me what being faithful and loving "till death do us part" mean. And he, a veteran of the U.S. Marine, took a stand for righteousness, even though it meant standing alone sometimes, and showed justice, fairness and equal respect to everyone he met

To my four loving children: Nadia, Gabrielle, Christopher and Olivia. You were patient and strong, and God allowed you to thrive in spite of the sacrifices that it took to complete this work.

To my readers: our struggles are real, but giving up is never an option!

Acknowledgements

I wish to personally thank the following people for their contributions to my inspiration and other help in producing this work:

The one who spoke the words of this book into existence, breathed life into it, formed it with care, cleansed it with love, and sent it forth in peace.

Alice Chung, who captured my vision perfectly to create the cover.

The men and women placed in my life at precise moments to inspire, pray, and to see this work to its completion, especially my church family!

And to the brave souls who take a stand for righteousness and share the message that God gives them, in spite of the sacrifice required.

Table of Contents

Introduction

*"I will praise thee; for I am fearfully and wonderfully made:
marvellous are thy works; and that my soul knoweth right well"*
— (PSALM 139:14 KING JAMES VERSION).

Every soul comes to Earth with a treasure and a purpose. Yet many of us refuse to live to our full potential. We are deceived into thinking that the things we see around us are all that exists. We focus on the illusions of our physical world, instead of training our spiritual eyes to focus on the hope of eternity. All the while, we rob humanity by not living, loving, giving, believing and serving as we ought to. In confusion, we turn on ourselves. In fear, we hate each other. And in ignorance, we fight the one who created us.

I wrestled with God for many years, believing that I was not good enough to write a book, and that he had somehow made a mistake in choosing me. In disobedience, I engaged in many projects that took my mind off of the idea of writing. I travelled the world, pursued a teaching career, and joined a religious movement that kept me preoccupied with the themes of 'world peace' and 'living carefree'.

I thought that I had succeeded in removing God's probing call from my mind. I was taught by the religious leaders of the group I was in that I had the power to make my life whatever I wanted it to be. So for a time, I thought that I was in control of my destiny and on the right path spiritually. But as time passed, none of these activities gave me the peace that I longed for. I became more and more discontent with life. And while everyone who knew me thought that I had it all together, I was anxious and constantly afraid of failure. Everything that I accomplished did not fill the void deep within my soul. And my anxiety climaxed one night in 2010.

There was a conflict that became the *last straw* that lead up to that night. I thought that what I am about to describe only happened in High School, but I was wrong. Four women at my job formed a clique, and because I did not believe in their values they made me a target. My cultural differences from the women became the main weapon of their attacks. Their rejection and their taunting grew more intense the more I tried to be strong. Life became unbearable! My good name, and everything else that I worked so hard to achieve, did not help my dilemma.

That night in 2010, I went to bed like I normally did. But I awoke around midnight, frustrated with the constant abuse that I faced at the hands of these women. I became aware of two dominant thoughts. One said, "You are not wanted and you are not loved. Life is not worth living." The other said, "You are loved more than you know, but you have to make the choice to believe God completely. Doubting some parts of God's words is not an option. You have to make the decision now to believe on your own."

I had never felt so alone and hopeless before. But that night I realized that I was in a real battle with a force that I could not see. I lay paralyzed in my bed because my weakened faith in God provided a means for that power to take control of my peace. Confusion filled my mind as I struggled to believe in a creator that I could not see or touch. I was overwhelmed! I wanted to believe, but I was dominated by the thought that one who created the heavens, the oceans, and everything else couldn't possibly care that much about me.

This battle in my mind went on for about an hour. Each time I tried to make the decision to believe God, I felt like something prevented me from doing so. I literally felt like I was being pulled away from a presence of pure love. As hard as it was for me to make a decision, it was that little spark of love that proved to me beyond a shadow of a doubt that there was something else out there: a beautiful presence of light- the Spirit of one who is in control, and who loves ME. I painfully and quietly submitted to God by whispering, "I believe." When I made the choice to believe completely that the Almighty God is higher and more powerful than any other force, a peace that I never felt before filled my soul. Right away, I opened my eyes and realized that I was up against something outside of myself- a power that was all about destroying me. But it was God's Spirit who offered me the option to live free in him.

That night, I came face to face, not with a god, but with the Most High God. He won that battle for me through his life giving Spirit, who we call the Holy Spirit. I knew then that I was more than just a woman. I was his daughter. I saw my chains of bondage fall off of me and I was set free. My soul is now free from the prison that I lived in, not just by those ladies' rejection, but from all those years living in ignorance of the love that God wants to share with me. People will do really mean things sometimes because they are ignorant of their own chains of bondage which are yanked to and fro by spiritual forces of wickedness. My life's purpose since 2010 has been to allow God to have total control of my life, and to keep those chains off of me as I share with others how they too can be set free from spiritual oppression.

In the Bible, Jesus shows us what it means to surrender totally to the Most High God. When I made the choice to believe in Jesus as a 13 year old, I did not fully understand all that that meant. But on that life-changing night in 2010, I came face to face with the power that is unleashed when we have even a little faith in the power of our heavenly father. God won the battle for me that night and he can win your battles too. Stop lying to yourself about the thoughts that oppress you. Face those thoughts with courage and believe that you were created to live free and in harmony with God. After you make the choice to live for him, the process of building and maintaining your faith is life-long. Some days will be harder than others. Just know that the benefits are abundant and spiritually liberating in every possible way. As each shackle falls off of us, our souls become freer and our eyes open wider to the greatness of God and the gift of our existence. We learn to guard that spiritual freedom at any cost, as our desire to live under the power, presence and peaceful personality of The Almighty is perfected!

My confession through a well of tears that night in 2010 was, "God, I don't understand everything the Bible says, but I choose tonight to believe everything." At that moment of faith, something changed. The very next day, I sat down with a pen and a notebook and asked the Most High to tell me what it is that he needs me to write. It was as if I turned on a faucet when I uttered that simple prayer, because the words have not stopped flowing since then. He showed me that we are each a wonderful and unique design created for a specific purpose, but that there are forces of wickedness that rob us of our blessings. While we go about life thinking that we can run from him and do whatever we want to, we are caught in the middle of a fierce and terrible battle for our souls.

When God opens your eyes you will wonder how you did not know all this time what was happening around you. If you are feeling down, he wants you to have a fulfilled life that you've never had before. If you are considering death, our heavenly father wants you to know that you will love life if you serve him faithfully. And if you think that our creator wants some of his children to die and some to live, know that he created us all to live eternally with him! But each of us must individually make the decision to believe and serve him completely.

This book mainly answers three of the questions we ask as human beings: Who created me? Who am I? And why was I created? It is written for anyone who feels, or has felt, depressed, rejected, bullied, or lacking in purpose at any time in their journey here on Earth. If you are a child of God, this book is for you!

This is not just a regular *self-help*, but will point you back to the Bible, and ask you to read and study the words of our creator for yourself. You might say, "I go to church and my preacher is responsible for studying the Word of God." If you have a place of worship, your religious leader is responsible for studying, and preparing sermons for you, but in order for the creator to work through your life, it is you who must allow these words to take root into your own soul by personally studying them. Imagine that your soul is an envelope and God wants you to read a message that he has inside. Just like you would open up an envelope to retrieve a message, the same way you have to make the effort to open up your soul to hear what he is telling you. I urge you to not just read, but to think deeply about the Bible verses given here. Please take time to study the passages of scripture for yourself! Develop a habit of memorizing God's Word, for it is the Word that guides and defends us against our daily battles.

As we study scripture, a clear picture will develop of who we really are: citizens and soldiers of God's kingdom. We are given all the resources that we need to do our heavenly father's work, and trained for spiritual warfare. Earth is not just our place of service, but our school as well. Our life experiences are lessons on how to refine the abilities that God has given to us. Our true warfare, while we are here, is not of the physical, but spiritual; for it is in our minds where the true battles of life are lost or won.

The spiritual forces of unrighteousness that dwell among us try to chain us down and keep us in bondage, preventing us from experiencing an abundant and spiritually liberated life. Do you want to be free from the shackles of sin that strive to destroy your soul? If you do, then you are in the right place. Put on God's whole armor and reclaim your soul's victory!

Part One

Who Created Me?

For thou hast possessed my reins: thou hast covered me in my mother's womb. I will praise thee; for I am fearfully and wonderfully made: marvellous are thy works; and that my soul knoweth right well. My substance was not hid from thee, when I was made in secret, and curiously wrought in the lowest parts of the earth. Thine eyes did see my substance, yet being unperfect; and in thy book all my members were written, which in continuance were fashioned, when as yet there was none of them. How precious also are thy thoughts unto me, O God! how great is the sum of them! If I should count them, they are more in number than the sand: when I awake, I am still with thee (Psalm 139:13-18).

One

LET'S START WITH A MAP!

"I am the door: by me if any man enters in, he shall be saved, and shall go in and out, and find pasture. The thief cometh not, but for to steal, and to kill, and to destroy: I am come that they might have life, and that they might have it more abundantly."

— (John 10:9-10).

I'm sure that you will agree that the best thing to do before going on a journey is to read the map on how to get to your destination. For this reason, we will consider a map that is given to us through the Word of God. This map will show us how to get to the straight and narrow road that takes us to our home in eternity. It is buried in the life, death and resurrection of Jesus Christ and can be found in the selection of passages that follow. As you read the following passages of scripture, I pray that you will see who you are- a sinner that needs to be reconciled to the creator. Secondly, I hope that you will believe that God sent his son into the world as a perfect sacrifice so that all of your sins will lose control over your life. Thirdly, I pray that you will accept Jesus Christ as our creator's saving grace, and as Jesus did, choose to surrender completely to

God's will. The verses below will explain clearly what all of this mean.

We begin the map to Salvation in chapter three of the book of Romans which tells us that we are all sinners and no one is perfectly righteous (Romans 3:10). This means that God knew us before he created us. It did not surprise him when Adam and Eve sinned, because he knew what they were capable of. You and I, and everyone else who descended from Adam and Eve, have inherited this nature of disobedience. Observing the ways of a young child shows us that we are all born wanting our own way, "for all have sinned, and come short of the glory of God" (Romans 3:23). Think on this verse for a moment, for many are convinced that their own righteousness, without giving God total control, pleases him and will lead to eternal life. No matter how holy someone thinks he/she is, all it takes is the perfect situation and that person will sin. To begin this journey, we must individually accept that sin separated us from God and that we need to re-submit our lives back to him in order to be fully restored. This is the starting point of our journey, and there is no other way for us to proceed to the next steps.

Our choice to sin, because of God's law of consequence, comes with a price, for the wages of sin is death (Romans 6:23). Notice that in everyday life, if something has a cost, you have to pay for it if you would like to have it. As descendants of Adam and Eve, we choose to sin, and so we must pay the cost. "But God commendeth his love toward us, in that, while we were yet sinners, Christ died for us" (Romans 5:8). A price was paid by our creator, and that was the sacrifice of Jesus. So, the price of sin is death, but the gift of God is eternal life through Christ Jesus our Lord (Romans 6:23). We must realize that Jesus was not just born by coincidence but as part of God's plan to reach out to a world condemned to death. As we shift our focus to the book of John, we are told that Jesus, who is also called the *Word*, existed in the beginning with God (John 1:2). Our wonderful creator had prepared a way back to himself from before time began, in spite of knowing the mistakes that we would make. This is the Good News!

Wouldn't you like to choose the path of eternal life that God prepared for us because of his unconditional love for us? We further read that if we declare with our mouths that Jesus is Lord, and believe in our hearts that God raised him from the dead, we will be saved. "For with the heart man believeth unto righteousness; and with the mouth confession is made unto salvation" (Romans 10:9-10). By believing in your heart and saying it with your mouth, you accept the gift of salvation and are saved from eternal hell. Upon believing and making this confession of faith, you may experience a peace that you have never felt before, which is sometimes your first conscious encounter with God's Holy Spirit. If you choose to accept God's salvation through Jesus Christ, you have entered the path of everlasting life, which you can never come off of again! Let us pray:

Dear God, Thank you for knowing the beginning and the end of all things. I am a sinner, but you sent Jesus Christ to save me. He died a terrible death for me. He was buried for me. He conquered death for me. You raised him from the dead and he is seated at your right hand, waiting for when you will declare the time for him to be united with me and all believers. I ask that you release the power of the Holy Spirit in my life. For the rest of my life, I ask you to search me, and know my heart, try me, and know my thoughts. See if there is any wicked way in me, and lead me in the way of everlasting life through Christ. I offer my life as a sacrifice back to you God, as a reasonable service for what you have done for me. Use me for your perfect will. Amen.

Now that you have accepted the free gift of salvation, know that the work is not done. If you just chose the way of Salvation through Jesus Christ, the rest of this book will make perfect sense. If you do not believe what you just read, keep reading. If you made the decision to follow Jesus Christ before having read this book, I am sure that the presentation of this message in the form of a road map was helpful as it was to me when my pastor explained it.

We are further instructed:

"For whosoever shall call upon the name of the Lord shall be saved. How then shall they call on him in whom they have not believed? and how shall they believe in him of whom they have not heard? and how shall they hear without a preacher?" (Romans 10:13-14).

This being said, we each have a responsibility to pass on the message about God's amazing grace and to share how his work through Jesus Christ has changed our lives.

I hope that you begin to see how important you are to God. Develop a new way of life of praise, worship and surrender to him! Daily thank him for his many blessings. And in every situation you find yourself in, ask him to show you the error of your ways. When he shows them to you, ask him to forgive and guide you in every way. When he guides you, obey!

What can you give God thanks for today?

What time(s) during the day can you devote to praying or studying God's Word?

Two

Don't Be Deceived!

"Who hath believed our report? and to whom is the arm of the LORD revealed? For he shall grow up before him as a tender plant, and as a root out of a dry ground: he hath no form nor comeliness; and when we shall see him, there is no beauty that we should desire him"

— (Isaiah 53:1-2).

We must now consider the false images which we've been led to believe are God and Jesus, perhaps causing many to draw further away from God. When we think of Jesus, a very common image comes up in our mind's eye. He is blond or brown haired, blue or brown eyed, long haired and delicate in his appearance. Jesus was a carpenter and we can all agree that carpenters are generally known for their rough appearance. We are also told in the introductory scripture from the book of Isaiah that there was nothing in Jesus' appearance that would make us desire him. Yet, mainstream media is filled with these flawlessly handsome images of Jesus. I read in the book of Revelations another interesting description of Jesus. It reads,

"And in the midst of the seven candlesticks one like unto the Son of man, clothed with a garment down to the foot, and girt about the paps with a golden girdle. His head and his hairs were white like wool, as white as snow; and his eyes were as a flame of fire; And his feet like unto fine brass, as if they burned in a furnace; and his voice as the sound of many waters" (Revelations 1:13-15).

Some might say that it is the color white that the word wool is describing, but if it was just the color the apostle John talks about, why didn't he only say "white like snow"? Wool is very significant because it applies to the hair type of a specific ethnic group. The reference to Jesus' feet having the color of fine brass that has been burnt in a furnace also paints a clear picture of Jesus' complexion. We have no reason in this age (generally referred to as the age of information) to say that we did not know the truth. We can research for ourselves and see the truth instead of accepting everything that we are told. Information about every topic can be found in the Bible, and that is why I have come to trust this book as my manual for life. But unfortunately, many are turned away from following God's words because they see some information presented in many religious circles as conflicting.

Some might say that what Jesus look like does not matter, or that I have misinterpreted the words of the Bible; but it does matter that we deal with the image that we think of as Jesus before we go any further. Thinking that the images presented as Jesus are really God's begotten son causes us to unconsciously allot the worship and prayer to an idol. And as the love and devotion to Jesus is allocated to this popular image, who many defend at all cost, we commit idolatry. I focus completely on what the Bible says since it represents the infallible truth of the Most High God. Am I saying then that we should create another image of Jesus with brown skin and wooly hair? Absolutely not! One of our creator's first commandments tells us not to make graven images or worship them. Also, none of us knows what Jesus and God really look like! This should be enough to put to rest the debate about what they look like, but the argument continues and becomes a stumbling block for many.

Some might argue that the above quoted verse in the book of Revelations is not enough to support my belief that Jesus could not be the image that we are taught to worship. So let us consider another fact from scripture: that God told Mary and Joseph to flee to Egypt to hide from King Herod. King Herod ordered the killing of all Israelite babies under the age of two years old to prevent Jesus' birth, since it was foretold that Jesus was destined to be a savior of the Jews (Matthew 2:1-15). A lot of information is published regarding the look of the ancient Egyptians, specifically during the time Jesus lived. The Egyptians were very much into preserving their possessions and their images; you can see this in the elaborate paintings found in the pyramids and tombs of Egypt. These works of art tell us that they were a brown skinned people. With this little background of the look of the Egyptians at the time of Jesus' birth, ask yourself this: why would God tell Joseph to escape to Egypt to hide Jesus if Jesus had the features of people we generally think of as European? How could a light skinned person with blue eyes (the image traditionally known to be Jesus) not stand out in Egypt, where most of the people, according to recent archaeological and DNA findings, were brown skinned?

At this point we must stop and ask the Most High to forgive us if we have worshipped these false images unknowingly. In order to continue on the path of finding out whose we are, we must renew our minds and not make or worship images of God or his son, Jesus Christ. We are warned:

I am the LORD thy God, which have brought thee out of the land of Egypt, out of the house of bondage. Thou shalt have no other gods before me. Thou shalt not make unto thee any graven image, or any likeness of anything that is in heaven above, or that is in the earth beneath, or that is in the water under the earth. Thou shalt not bow down thyself to them, nor serve them: for I the LORD thy God am a jealous God, visiting the iniquity of the fathers upon the children unto the third and fourth generation of them that hate me (Exodus 20:1-4).

The fact that God chose this as the first commandment to give his people should tell us how important it is to him that we do not make images and worship them. Many times we naturally fall into the pattern of worshiping the popular images of Jesus and God and we must stop. How can we have any real power if we continue to offer our prayers to an idol that has no life, or never existed? May God forgive us and heal our minds before we try to start a new life in him.

What image comes to your mind when you think of God or Jesus?

Ask God today to renew your mind, and heal you from all unrighteousness. Make a note of any inspiration you receive.

Three

Our Creator-The Most High God

"For thou hast possessed my reins: thou hast covered me in my mother's womb. I will praise thee; for I am fearfully and wonderfully made: marvellous are thy works; and that my soul knoweth right well. My substance was not hid from thee, when I was made in secret, and curiously wrought in the lowest parts of the earth. Thine eyes did see my substance, yet being unperfect; and in thy book all my members were written, which in continuance were fashioned, when as yet there was none of them"

— (Psalm 139:13-16).

Our creator, who occupies the heavens, the Earth, and all that is, knows us by name, knows every hair on our heads, and has a presence within each of us. Today, we find it hard to wrap our minds around the way we began our existence in this world; yet here we are living, breathing, thinking beings. In our attempt to answer the age-old questions of who we are and why we are alive, we must first delve into the question of whose we are. The Bible says that mankind's history began in the garden of Eden with Adam and Eve, and that when they were created, God declared, "Let us make man in our image, after our likeness: and let them have dominion over the fish of the sea, and over the fowl of the air, and over the cattle, and over all the earth, and over every creeping thing that creepeth upon the earth" (Genesis 1:26). This is a very powerful passage that should tell us that God created us to be like him. When most of us think of our creator, we usually think of a ruler, and not as a parent who wants to have a relationship with each of us.

Many church goers' relationship with God stop at their reverence of Jesus as their "personal Lord and Savior", but even Jesus recognized one greater than himself, whom he called "our father which art in heaven" (Matthew 6:9). He said that he and the father are one, and he prayed to a father, but he never said 'I am the father'. It is clear to me that "I am the father" and "I and the father are one" mean two different things. If Jesus had said, "I am the father," that would mean that Jesus is supreme and there is no higher power than himself. But when Jesus said, "I and my father are one," he means that he is completely representative of his father in his image, his message and his works. He is the perfect image of the father, but not the father. I know that this is a tough concept to grasp. But as with every other detail presented in this book, I urge you to ask God to give you a deeper understanding of it. We too were made in the perfect image of the father. Aren't we told that our bodies are temples of the living God? (1 Corinthians 6:19). We are currently not functioning at our fullest potential as God's children. But Jesus did! And when he said that to see him was to see the father, he was talking about his real self on the inside, and not his physical body. When he taught his followers how to pray, he showed, in no uncertain terms, that we share the same parent.

At first, I was frustrated because it was difficult for me to wrap my mind around this concept of God being a father. But one evening as I was at a ladies' meeting, my pastor's wife gave a message that transformed me and gave me the insight to complete this chapter. The main idea of her message was about us seeing God as our father. She told us, "God is not just our creator, he is our father and we need to reverence him as a father." She also said that when she prays, she sometimes calls God: "Daddy". Her simple message made a profound impact on me. I felt so guilty when I realized that I thought of our creator only as "God" and not as one who is also my parent. Because of this distant idea that I had of our heavenly father, it was hard to overcome many struggles that I had experienced in the past.

The very next day I woke up and tried to pray to God as my father, but I did not know what to say. I was speechless, still struggling to see him as a father. All I could do was say, "Thank you, Father." I repented for every time I felt weak and did not realize that I had a heavenly father who created everything and controls everything. I felt guilty of the many opportunities I missed to rely on my father's protective embrace, instead of remaining shackled to my problems and giving in to my fears. I made up my mind then that I was going to work harder at knowing God as my father and not just as a sovereign ruler of creation.

If you could talk to God as your father, what would you tell him? Write him a letter and be as honest as you can be.

Four

The Mysterious Ways of The Most High

"Trust in the LORD with all thine heart; and
lean not unto thine own understanding"
— (PROVERBS 3:5).

There are times when we reach a spiritual high in our journey, and we get the feeling that we understand fully what God is about. It's a season when we are in harmony with his plans for our lives. Then after this short period of rest, a new situation arises and we find our faith freshly being challenged. We interpret these tests as "bad days", but are they really that? We must learn to see all of our situations as pages of life that have the potential to teach us more about ourselves and our creator. When we experience any hardship, it would be wise to follow these steps. First, we must pray and thank God for the good that he expects to come from that situation. Next we must ask him to give us the power to forgive the offender, and ask him to forgive us of our sins. Then we need to ask him to show us how we should react. Our minds cannot fully grasp the way our creator works because some of what he allows into our lives bring much pain. But we MUST realize that all of our experiences serve a divine purpose. Thanking God, asking him to take full control, and obeying his guidance will strengthen our relationship with him. We will begin to see patterns and realize that his work in our lives is actually very systematic.

There are times when we will question God when life gets unbearable. We will wonder why he had to choose us to have that experience instead of someone else, who we feel deserves it. If we ask him these questions in humility and respect of his power, he will answer us. He may use vivid memories of the past- memories that we may not want to deal with. He might use dreams to let us know what steps we must take. God also speaks directly through his Word and through the people who are in our lives when answering our questions. If we don't pay close attention we will miss out on these messages. The answers may not be what we expect, and it is only when we have a close relationship with our heavenly father that we can tell if those answers come from him or not. The ability to tell whether or not an instruction comes from God is called discernment. I urge you then to ask him for the gift of spiritual discernment today.

For us to make the best out of life, we must know that we cannot rely on our own limited human understanding. Why? Because our understanding is based on conclusions made from our experiences in the past. The best *you* that you could ever be happens when you turn all power over to God and depend on his every word right here in the present. We cannot change the activities of our past, but we can revisit our past with his help, and re-evaluate and reinterpret those experiences based on truth. It is only then that we can continue the process of freeing our souls. As we revisit the past and take from it the lessons that God would have us take, we use these truths to build the person we are today. To excel in the present we must refuse to react in ways that failed us in the past, and not for a second trust our own understanding again. Instead, we must trust in our heavenly father with all of our heart in thanksgiving, all of our soul with worship, and with all of our minds in total surrender to him. The constant preoccupation of our minds should be, "Father, what must I do for you now?"

What painful situations have you experienced in your past?

How did these experiences impact your life?

What difficult relationships or situations do you have in your life at this time?

How do you react to these situations or people now?

Five

DIVINE LAWS

"God that made the world and all things therein, seeing that he is Lord of heaven and earth, dwelleth not in temples made with hands; Neither is worshiped with men's hands, as though he needed anything, seeing he giveth to all life, and breath, and all things; And hath made of one blood all nations of men for to dwell on all the face of the earth, and hath determined the times before appointed, and the bounds of their habitation..." — (ACTS 17:24-26).

All of creation, whether on Earth, in the heavens or in the seas, is governed by a set of laws which will stay the same for eternity. No matter the color, culture or country of a person, these set of laws or principles govern all of us. They are sometimes referred to as *Principles of Truth*. We will look at seven of these principles which are necessary for us to know who God is and what we mean to him. Understanding how they work will correctly equip us to win spiritual battles and enable us to stand confidently in the twists and turns of life. Our creator is divine because he is perfection in every way. All of his creation is therefore a representation of this perfect, divine and orderly creator. We are told in the Bible that God is spirit, and everyone who worships him must worship him in spirit and in truth (John 4:24). If we do not know God's law, or what is truth, how can we defend ourselves and follow his command in spiritual warfare? It is very important then that we know the principles which make up this truth so that we can truly worship our divine creator in spirit.

I would like to note here that many usually think of God's commandments as laws, and his principles as truths. So to not confuse the reader, we will use the words law, laws, truth and truths interchangeably. Just know that all of the laws of God come together to make up the complete **law** of his creation; and when I say truths, I mean the principles of **truth**; for there is only one law and one truth. All of his commandments work as one. The principles of truth that we will learn in this book are: divine order, divine trinity, divine forgiveness, divine humility, divine love, divine harmony, and divine consequence.

Based on your observation alone, what cycles or patterns do you see common to nature? (Consider how the animals, plants, and other elements found in nature function in harmony.)

Six

DIVINE ORDER

"A man's heart deviseth his way: but the LORD directeth his steps"
— (PROVERBS 16:9)

*W*hen a baby is born, it has the perfect will of the creator embedded in its innermost being. Each physical experience that our creator has planned for that soul has already been laid out. The people that this soul will encounter, the places the person will go to, and the decisions that God would like this soul to make have all been planned out ahead of time. If you are not convinced, let us revisit a passage from the previous chapter:

God that made the world and all things therein, seeing that he is Lord of heaven and earth, dwelleth not in temples made with hands; Neither is worshiped with men's hands, as though he needed anything, seeing he giveth to all life, and breath, and all things; And hath made of one blood all nations of men for to dwell on all the face of the earth, and hath determined the times before appointed, and the bounds of their habitation..." (Acts 17:24-26).

Lines four to six tell us that the times of our lives, and where we will live, are appointed before any of these things happen to us. You might ask: if every physical aspect of our lives has been pre-determined by our creator, then what's the point to living? This is an excellent question! The answer to this question is summed up in the opening scripture above, "A man's heart deviseth his way: but the LORD directeth his steps" (Proverbs 16:9).

Before I give an explanation, let me point out that man has tried for ages to understand and give a name to the real us who lives inside of the body. Some say the real us is in our hearts. Others say the real us is our mind. Many say the real us is our soul. And there are those who say it is our spirit. These are the words that we use in English alone. Imagine how many more words are there to define the real *us* in the thousands of other languages that exist. Let me say then that I believe that there is only one you and one me. We are confused by all of these terms that society uses, but no matter where you go, who you meet, or how your body changes, there is a real you on the inside. Have you ever planted a seed, and noticed that a dead layer falls off of it leaving a living embryo on the inside? This is what develops roots and grows upward as a new plant. The dry shell you see on the outside of a seed is not the seed, but just the covering of the seed. The true seed is dormant, but perfectly alive within the shell. It's the same way we are. When the shell, which is our physical body, decays, our soul can be fully expressed and returns to its maker.

The real us is spiritual; this means that the real us cannot be seen with our naked eyes. The real, spiritual, you and me, have spiritual organs that match the physical organs in our physical bodies. This book mainly deals with three of these spiritual organs. They are the mind or will which matches the brain, the emotional center which matches our heart, and the soul, the spiritual skin which closes in around all of our spiritual organs and filters the thoughts that go in and come out. The physical match of the soul is the skin of the human body. Whether you believe this or not, this is what our heavenly father revealed to me and I know that this message is true. For the purpose of this book, I will use the terms 'mind and will', 'emotional center and heart', and 'soul and all of our being' interchangeably.

With the real you simplified, let us look again at the scripture from Proverbs. When it says that a man's heart deviseth his way, it means that our emotional center influences our mind and fuels our soul; it is our emotions that help us decide how we will interpret our experiences. The emotions influence the will to think, to plan, and to interpret the situations of life. And when it says that the LORD directeth man's steps, it means that nothing is a coincidence or happens because we planned for it to happen that way. The truth, as revealed in this passage in the book of Acts, is that God manages the situations that we encounter.

His workers, who we call angels, are in the midst of us working out God's divine order. They set the stage of our day to day lives, put people together, formulate plots, prepare our lines and organize the problems and solutions of our time here on Earth. However, God has given us choices in the midst of his plans. Each day, we live in two worlds. One of these is the physical one, in which we are placed in specific situations with people and things that we see and interact with. The second world is what we call the spiritual, in which our souls function with other spiritual beings behind the scenes. It is in our spiritual world that we decide how we will respond to people's actions and interpret situations that we are placed in. It is in the spiritual realm where we choose whether or not we will surrender our will to the will of the Most High God. We are taught that we have many choices, but in the spiritual there are only two choices in every situation: the choice to obey and the choice to disobey God. Our thought life is what many call the spiritual realm. However, our will and our emotional center are also organs that operate in the spiritual realm.

Moment by moment, we wrestle and strive between thoughts of obedience and those of disobedience against God. There is a presence, which we usually refer to as *the devil*, which is at work around us, spurring us on to sin against the Most High's natural order. The Bible calls this force "the enemy" and "spiritual powers of wickedness in high places". For every good plan that God has for us, the enemy has one to corrupt our spiritual life and turn us away from God. We must always be aware of this force and keep the lines of communication with our heavenly father open. We are told:

> Rejoice evermore. Pray without ceasing. In everything give thanks: for this is the will of God in Christ Jesus concerning you. Quench not the Spirit. Despise not prophesyings. Prove all things; hold fast that which is good. Abstain from all appearance of evil. And the very God of peace sanctify you wholly; and I pray God your whole spirit and soul and body be preserved blameless unto the coming of our Lord Jesus Christ. Faithful is he that calleth you, who also will do it (I Thessalonians: 5:16-24).

This powerful message sums up many essential points about how we are to live during our journey here on Earth.

Many of society's teachings corrupt our minds from a very early age about what our purpose on Earth is. We learn to look to our spiritual leaders as the only means of finding out what is our purpose, and forget to personally connect to the one source who knows all and is all. Our lives then become meaningless as we wander from day to day, deceived to dwell on the past, or to aimlessly plan for the future. We find that none of this fills the void or unravels the confusion in our souls. In order to find our true worth, we must first cleanse our minds of what we were taught and ask the creator to renew our minds and show us truth. When we insist on returning to the things that God has cleansed from our lives, we are like an animal who returns to its vomit! We must stop vomiting back up the past as if it could make us better in any way. Instead, it would be wise to see the errors of our past for what they are: forbidden vomit that must only be handled with God's guidance, then quickly set aside and quarantined. We cannot live in the present and past at the same time. Seek

God's help if you are constantly going back to your past instead of abundantly living in your present.

We need to set out to chew on the truth of the Word of God, and feast on the lessons that Jesus taught about how to truly live this life. We must ask ourselves: how much of what I know is because someone else said so? Of all the knowledge that I have, which can I say came from God directly? Has he revealed these things to me through his Word, or are they second-hand information? Many of the messages and images that we receive in this life *mixes things up* in our minds and give us a weakened or corrupted knowledge of who we are and what we are doing here on Earth. In order to truly see, we must step out of everything that is happening around us and dwell in the spirit with our heavenly father on a personal level (John 4:24).

As we just learned, God already knew what would have become of each of his creation. There is enough evidence in the Bible alone that shows us this. He even knew when our birthdays would be, and that is why people who study the zodiac and astrology swear that it works. Our heavenly father created the heavenly hosts, and strung them together in perfect alignment to give us signs and seasons (Genesis 1:14-19). Many of my readers might find my example about the Zodiac as an uncomfortable subject. However, I have two points to make here about the zodiac and astrology. First, the phenomenal creations in the sky above us can truly be studied because they were made to function with order and harmony with the rest of creation. Second, instead of paying someone to tell us what God says, we must each strive to maintain a close relationship with him so that we will live according to his will for our lives. I do not believe in looking to an astrologer or fortune teller to tell me what God wants. If he has to constantly use someone to speak to me, it's because I am not listening to him. If that is the case, shouldn't I pay more attention to him instead of paying someone else to listen for me?

Nothing is by coincidence. Ask yourself this, how chaotic would it be if it was left up to chance for all the atoms, molecules, oceans, animals, people, plants, and planets to just do whatever they wanted to do. Try to visualize it. Nothing would last longer than seconds operating in this chaos, except in chaos, because chaos can only create more chaos. Yet we are taught in modern science that things occurred in chaos for billions of years until they just started to work themselves out to create the order that we have today. But as we observe nature around us we see that there is an order to everything. If chaos created order, why isn't there still some chaos left to be put in order?

All of nature, which was created by God, reflects order, and there is a combination of laws that they all follow. Because of our free will, man has struggled with obedience since Eden, and this has caused us to be in disharmony with the rest of creation. God continues to remind us of his laws, as with Moses and the Israelites in the Old Testament of the Bible, with the goal of bringing us back to the harmonious relationship we once had with him. He already knows that some will obey him and others will not. But he gives us his law anyway. The choice has to be made by each one of us as to how we will respond to him. We are programed by our society to believe that if we think it, we create it, and that everything that happens around us is because of what we think in our minds. This is partly true. We have experiences to make us spiritually mature, so that we will be more and more like our creator. But nothing happens outside of God's control. His main goal is for his children to be like him, and so nothing happens to us unless he approves of it.

This might seem difficult to understand because we were taught the opposite all our lives. Consider this: God knowing what is in our thoughts (Psalm 139:2-4) plans out our lives so that each individual soul will be given the chance to have eternal life with him. His goal is to make us perfect! Jesus says, "Be ye perfect, even as your Father which is in heaven is perfect" (Matthew 5:48). Therefore, brothers and sisters, everything that unfolds in this life is to make our souls perfectly dedicated to God. While living on Earth, Jesus' spirit was in perfect union with God's spirit, because he was perfectly obedient to him. Notice that this perfection is of the soul, not of our physical body. And God is the judge of our perfection, not man. We cannot judge each other's dedication to God because we cannot see the total dimensions of someone's soul.

Some might wonder if the terrors that some children face at the hands of adults are also a part of God's plan. These things were not a part of his initial plan for us because he did not create us to sin. But when he saw what we were capable of because of our freewill, he created an order around our actions, and planned a way for all of his children to be reconciled back to him in spite of our experiences. I am not saying that our actions do not cause other reactions. Neither am I saying that our creator allows things to happen in people's lives because he is unfair. God has made life fair through him, and it is only through surrendering our lives to him that we can see his hidden love in the midst of the terrors we face.

Let us think about some other teachings of Jesus for a moment. He taught us that our bodies produce the works caused by sin. But if we allow God's Spirit to grow in us, our lives will reveal its fruit, which is not of our body or our flesh, but of God's own Spirit. Paul, a follower of Jesus wrote,

> Idolatry, witchcraft, hatred, variance, emulations, wrath, strife, seditions, heresies, Envyings, murders, drunkenness, revellings, and such like: of the which I tell you before, as I have also told you in time past, that they which do such things shall not inherit the kingdom of God. But the fruit of the Spirit is love, joy, peace, longsuffering, gentleness, goodness, faith, Meekness, temperance: against such there is no law. And they that are Christ's have crucified the flesh with the affections and lusts. If we live in the Spirit, let us also walk in the Spirit (Galations 5:20-25).

As the fruit of the Spirit is matured in you by the various manifestations listed above, your body will no longer be controlled by the works of the flesh. I am not saying that you will not make mistakes. But when the Spirit is bearing fruit in you, you will find that your vulnerability to sin gradually dies. Our souls experience a newness of life, transformed to the likeness of Christ, and we are refined and prepared for everlasting life.

In the first part of the passage in Galations that deals with things that are against God's Spirit, we see the words "works of the flesh". Notice that it didn't say fruit of the flesh, but works of the flesh. The flesh is used to "work". And no matter how much work it does, it cannot produce the fruit of God's Spirit. It is how our souls respond to these works that determines our growth in the 'fruit of the spirit'. The growth and production of the fruit of the spirit happens in our soul, through our choice of obedience to God. For example, you might be at work one day and get into an argument with your co-worker. That incident had already been planned out before you were born. But the way you respond in your mind to this incident is entirely up to you. What everyone involved in that experience learns, and how each one grows from the encounter, was the purpose of the argument. God allowed the incident to happen in order to cause the parties involved to grow in a specific quality of the fruit of the spirit. All of this is in his perfect, divine order.

We call some things *bad* and others *good*. God calls everything: divine order. Therefore shame, hate and unforgiveness are not the truth but lies that we choose to accept as true; these lies destroy the protective shield of our soul little by little, and create many more open doors for spiritual attack. When we entertain the thoughts that tell us that our sins and the sins of others cannot be forgiven, or that we should live in regret for our past actions, we carry around a heavy load of untruths that conflict with God's principles of truth. The burden that we take on is great and come in all forms of mental and emotional issues that were never meant to be carried. Instead, we must continually ask our heavenly father to show us how to live free in the present moment.

God wants us to know that every encounter is an opportunity to develop a closer relationship with him. This will in turn make us look more and more like his image. He wants us to be like him!

He wants us to love like he loves, see like he sees, and to have life in him. But all of this does not happen by each of us doing our own thing and disobeying him. Our ability to be like God only comes through our complete surrender to his will. We surrender completely to him by humbly approaching him for guidance in every moment of our lives. This is not a one-time thing, but a work in progress until, by his standard, we are perfectly aligned to the image he originally had for us. Let us each then rededicate our lives back to God.

How does this lesson on divine order change the way you think about your life?

What difficulty or illness do you have now that makes life seem unfair or out of order?

List past experiences of your life in which you've never asked God for guidance.

List your current challenges that you've never asked God for guidance in.

What challenges are you still struggling with, in spite of asking God for guidance?

Use this space to write a note to your heavenly father, asking him for guidance in how to correctly interpret the traumas or challenges of your past.

Use this space to write a note to your heavenly father, asking him for guidance in how to correctly interpret the traumas and challenges of your life today.

$\mathcal{S}$even

THE DIVINE TRINITY

*For there are three that bear record in heaven, the Father, the
Word, and the Holy Ghost: and these three are one*
— (1 John 5:7).

$\mathcal{W}$ hen I first tried to understand the trinity of God, I visual-
ized our creator split into thirds of a circle with one third
being God, one third being the Holy Spirit and one third being
Jesus. Thinking of the trinity in this way made it very confusing.
The Holy Spirit introduced me to the three natures of God by giv-
ing me a practical example that I can relate to: the trunk, leaves
and seed of a coconut tree. Anyone that lives in close contact with
a coconut tree knows that this is a very resourceful plant and its
parts are used for many things. For the purpose here, we will only
look at the trunk, the leaves and the seed.

The trunk represents the all-encompassing will of God-the fa-
ther, who has his roots buried in the Earth, and the rest of creation
extending into the universe. As with any tree, it is the trunk that
determines the identity of the other parts of the plant. The trunk
of a coconut tree is very straightforward and robust in its appear-
ance! And like all trunks, all it seems to do is to hold everything

else in place. But there is more to the trunk that we cannot see. As we will find out, it's not about what we can't see, but what we cannot live without. What would a coconut tree, or any other tree for that matter, look like without its trunk? The trunk signifies the sovereignty of God the father. Without the Most High God, the creator and father of all, nothing would be held up, because it is by his will and divine order that everything was called into being. Just as the root and trunk of the coconut tree lead to the production of its leaves and seeds, the same way the son and the Holy Spirit are manifestations of God the father.

Let us shift our attention to the significance of the leaves. The long branches of a coconut tree extend from the trunk and form bountiful sections of long, thin leaves. These leaves represent the life that is given to all of God's creation. This life which he breathes into us is his Holy Spirit. The leaves of a coconut tree are like other palm trees: their length and texture make their uses many and diverse. The sky is the limit as to what you can do with the leaves from a coconut tree. In Guyana, these leaves are used to make brooms, kites, and a wide variety of basket crafts. If you are caught in the rain, you can even shelter under these palms, as they are called. Just as the uses of the leaves of a coconut tree are many and varied, and depend upon the knowledge of the user, the same way the function of the Holy Spirit is limitless, and depends upon the liberty that each person gives it.

Now let's look at the coconut seed and see how it can be compared to the son (otherwise known as the Word) of God. It is natural to think that the coconut is a fruit or a nut because of its name, but the coconut is known as a seed in Guyana. This seed is dried and then replanted to become a new coconut plant. How does the coconut seed compare to the Son of God? Just as a coconut tree produces coconuts, which can then be planted to create a new tree, the same way the Son (Word) of God is planted and re-planted, continually adding to God's kingdom. We therefore must be careful how we use the *word* (the power of speech), because our words are seeds also, which when uttered have the power to create. Our words will manifest truth if we are completely surrendered to God's will. And our words will create lies if we are not in obedience to God. These lies can seem very real to us because thoughts are real. But even though these lies are real in our minds, that still does not make them truth.

We have already seen in previous chapters that thoughts and emotions are real but cannot be seen because they exist in the spiritual realm. But even though we cannot see them, we can feel their impact. Therefore, we must be careful how we entertain the thoughts and emotions that flow within us. The best thing we can do for ourselves is to ask God daily to take full control of our use of the word (the power of speech). When God is in control, all will be well because he will show us how to use his Word to create in his divine order.

Why is it necessary to know the three manifestations of God? If we do, we will get a clearer picture of the completeness of God. We will know that he is able, and has all the power, to do everything that he says he will do with his creation. This foundation will in turn build our faith in him during our daily battles, as we see that our creator is not out of touch, but in absolute control. Finally, getting a grasp on the trinity of God will better develop our knowledge of who we are.

How does this teaching on the holy trinity help you to understand God better?

How does this teaching on the holy trinity help you to understand yourself better?

Eight

DIVINE FORGIVENESS

Then came Peter to him, and said, Lord, how oft shall my brother sin against me, and I forgive him? till seven times? Jesus saith unto him, I say not unto thee, Until seven times: but, Until seventy times seven. Therefore is the kingdom of heaven likened unto a certain king, which would take account of his servants. And when he had begun to reckon, one was brought unto him, which owed him ten thousand talents. But forasmuch as he had not to pay, his lord commanded him to be sold, and his wife, and children, and all that he had, and payment to be made. The servant therefore fell down, and worshipped him, saying, Lord, have patience with me, and I will pay thee all. Then the lord of that servant was moved with compassion, and loosed him, and forgave him the debt. But the same servant went out, and found one of his fellow servants, which owed him an hundred pence: and he laid hands on him, and took him by the throat, saying, Pay me that thou owest. And his fellow servant fell down at his feet, and besought him, saying, Have patience with me, and I will pay thee all. And he would not: but went and cast him into prison, till he should pay the debt. So when his fellow servants saw what was done, they were very sorry, and came and told unto their lord all that was done. Then his lord, after that he had called him, said unto him, O thou wicked servant, I forgave thee all that debt, because thou desiredst me: Shouldest not thou also have had compassion on thy fellow servant, even as I had pity on thee? And his lord

was wroth, and delivered him to the tormentors, till he should pay all that was due unto him. So likewise shall my heavenly Father do also unto you, if ye from your hearts forgive not everyone his brother their trespasses
— (MATTHEW 18:21-35).

*T*he above passage shows a very serious lesson that must be learned if we are to live in a way that pleases the Most High God. It tells us that the only way to grow spiritually, or to develop a close relationship with God, is to be a master of forgiveness. But we find it difficult to let go of the *wrong* done to us, even though we expect to be forgiven for the *wrongs* that we do. When we have this struggle, we let our emotions control our will instead of letting our will control our emotions. Saying, "I forgive you," is not forgiveness. Forgiveness is a day to day choice of saying NO to the thoughts and emotions that tell us that we have a true interpretation of what was done to us, and that we are in our right to punish others for causing us pain. Forgiveness is a perfect show of God's love, where we honestly, and without emotion, face the action that someone did and ask the Most High to show us what the correct response is. His laws are in place to execute the perfect effect for every action, so we never need to worry that this person will somehow escape judgement. Forgiveness is the key to entering the kingdom because we show that we have truly humbled our will to God, and know that everything that happens is in his perfect will.

Jesus says that the kingdom of heaven *is* compared to a king who takes account of his servants. This means that God checks on us from time to time to see what is in our hearts! He keeps track of our growth through his Holy Spirit and through his many angels who constantly keep watch over us. Jesus is saying clearly that this process where God searches our hearts is a continuous one that we should be aware of whenever we judge people's actions. When our heavenly father sees that we are not forgiving, he allows difficult situations to plague our lives until we master the skill of forgiveness. Why is forgiveness so important? We see from the story above about the unforgiving servant that the law of forgiveness is a two-way street, in that if we do not forgive, we cannot be forgiven. We forgive others to make a way for the forgiveness of our own sins. When we don't forgive, the path to our own sins is not reached. We cannot have full healing and we are "tortured" by our desire to seek vengeance. When we do not forgive we give that person's sin power, declaring that it is too great to fall under God's power. In calling their sin unforgiveable we call our own sin unforgiveable, because as we learned earlier, we are all connected, and sin is sin. Jesus summed up the importance of this law when he taught us how to pray by asking our heavenly father to forgive us of our sins as we forgive those who sin against us (Matthew 6:12). We cannot expect God to hear our prayers when he sees unforgiveness in our hearts (our emotional center).

Let us look at what forgiveness is NOT:
Forgiveness is not:

1. the absence of pain.
2. for the person forgiven.
3. simply telling someone you forgive them.
4. reminding yourself of your faults.
5. reminding others of their past offenses.
6. secretly seeking retribution for a wrong done.
7. avoiding your community's system of justice.
8. a one time, or periodic thing.

It is important for us to know this principle of God's law because if you violate one principle of the law, you violate the whole law. With the above eight points out in the open, let us cleanse our minds from the untruths we have learned by asking our creator to fill us with the true meaning of forgiveness.

Jesus told the above story as part of his answer to Peter's question about how many times he should forgive someone who offends him. With his question, Peter was demonstrating to Jesus what he learned before about forgiveness- that seven times was enough times to forgive (Matthew 18:21). Jesus told him a much greater number- seventy times seven times, which when calculated is four hundred ninety times for just one offense. Did Jesus mean this literally? My friends, the message that Jesus is sharing with us is that forgiveness is an ongoing action. Who in their right mind stands around long enough to commit one offence, or to count someone's offense, four hundred and ninety times? What about the other offenses that will be made by that same person? And what about the other offenses by the thousands of other people who make up our lives? Jesus shows us with this lesson that someone who offends or hurts us might keep doing so over and over again. Because of this we each need to determine in our minds that we WILL forgive, and choose to make it a natural part of our daily life. This does not mean that this person will not face the consequences of his/her actions. Forgiveness is what you do internally to release that person to God so that you can keep on loving and living abundantly in spite of what that person does to you.

Forgiveness keeps us grounded in the present, and makes us able to focus on what God is doing through us at the present time. It puts us in the right mindset to enjoy what he is doing NOW. When you truly forgive, you say:

> "I am not what someone else did to me, and I am not what their actions tempt me to be. I refuse to think about how their actions hurt me. I will not base my love for them on their sin history. Hope, faith and prayer is the answer, for there is much more to things that I can see. I am too busy finding out what in the present moment God wants me to be!"

Forgiveness has such a regenerative power that healing naturally flows while performing it. It is therefore the vehicle by which God's love, power and mercy are transmitted among us. Forgiveness comes from a mind/will which says, "Father, I know that you allowed this situation into my life for some form of learning to take place. Let it transform me into what you want me to be. Have your way!" Unconditional love leads to forgiveness, and true forgiveness shows the true love of God. Forgiveness was a big part of Jesus' ministry, and he often invoked its power when he healed the sick.

As with any of the spiritual laws, practicing forgiveness does not just happen. We must ask God to teach us how. When we do, he will show us the people who we have allowed to *get under our skin,* and the burdens of our past that we are still carrying. He will invite us to give them over to him, as his shoulders are wide enough to carry them all. We are to let God show us the lessons that we are supposed to learn from our hurts. This requires patience, open-mindedness, and a willingness on our part to make drastic changes in how we think. God sees everything and he is a righteous judge, so all offenders of his law will face the consequences of their actions, even when they are forgiven. Let us therefore be very careful in what we think, say and do. We can choose to accept and practice the power of forgiveness. Or we can choose to believe that forgiving people is unfair, and continue to be tormented in our own souls for the wrongs that we ourselves do.

Who do you find hard to forgive?

Gillian Herman-Davis

What is stopping you from forgiving this/these person(s)?

What actions from your past, or your life today, do you think is unforgiveable? Tell God and ask him to forgive you.

42

Meditate on this verse: "Create in me a clean heart, O God; and renew a right spirit within me" (Psalm 51:10). And pray as the Spirit leads.

Now ask God to show you truth in these situations and teach you how to forgive.

What does God expect you to learn from those past hurts?

What does he expect you to learn from your current challenges?

Nine

DIVINE HUMILITY

Blessed are the poor in spirit: for theirs is the kingdom of heaven. Blessed are they that mourn: for they shall be comforted. Blessed are the meek: for they shall inherit the earth. Blessed are they which do hunger and thirst after righteousness: for they shall be filled. Blessed are the merciful: for they shall obtain mercy. Blessed are the pure in heart: for they shall see God. Blessed are the peacemakers: for they shall be called the children of God. Blessed are they which are persecuted for righteousness' sake: for theirs is the kingdom of heaven. Blessed are ye, when men shall revile you, and persecute you, and shall say all manner of evil against you falsely, for my sake

— *(MATTHEW 5:3-11).*

As we've learned, all experiences here on Earth fits into God's master plan for his creation based on what he prepared for us before he gave us life. Divine humility is when we come to the point of acceptance that all is God's and that our only purpose is to obey him. When we come to this place where we know that we have been created by one much greater than ourselves, for his will alone, we will reach the point of divine humility. But this is not easy to accomplish; we are bombarded from the time we awake each day by thoughts, and the media, which tell us that we can always improve on ourselves by our own devices. There is also a very popular religion in our world today which gives us a close but different teaching about humility; it teaches that evil exists only in our mind, and that we must seek world peace through looking for the good in every person. This to them is the foundation of humility. This is a very close teaching to the words of God but not totally true. We cannot achieve perfection through our own abilities alone. The truth is that we can only achieve perfection through the choice of humbling ourselves to the will of God. We do this by believing that he is the only God, that he sent his son, Jesus Christ, as the perfect sacrifice for our sins, and by following the way of self-sacrifice and dedication to his will.

I will not mention the name of this religion or any other religion in this work because bashing religions is not the purpose of this work. We sometimes get too caught up in arguments over cultural practices, when we should only be focused on sharing the true knowledge of God's Word and on worshiping him. True religion is a personal thing that is between a person and the creator. It happens in our souls!

True religion is humbling our will to the Most High God, and seeking his guidance in every aspect of our lives. This book is about presenting the Word of God and educating the reader about the power that lies dormant within each of God's children, which is awakened when we give our lives back to him.

Jesus taught us what true religion means with the example of his own life. He focused on being humble and gave us a list of the qualities that are vital to worshiping the Most High God. This list was given in Jesus' famous "Sermon on the Mount" and generally known as "The B' Attitudes". Let's have a look to see how we can take on each of these attitudes in our daily lives so that we can truly be humble.

"Blessed are the poor in spirit: for theirs is the kingdom of heaven" (Matthew 5:3).

As we ask God to take control of our will, our desire to control our situation shrinks. And as we become poor in spirit, we become rich in the powerful manifestation of God's Spirit. People will see the blessings that show up in our lives and marvel at our achievements, while we will praise God knowing that it was only through his guidance that we became successful. Jesus shows us here that those who surrender their lives to God will become poor in their own strength, but abundantly strengthened and motivated through his Spirit to live this life and be prepared for eternity.

"Blessed are they that mourn: for they shall be comforted" (5:4).

An inevitable part of following the way of Jesus Christ on the narrow road to eternal life is mourning. No matter what we do, we cannot escape the sadness that comes from living righteously in God's kingdom. Our spiritual eyes become open and we begin to see the strongholds of sin. We mourn when we try to teach others the truth and they won't listen. Later when these same people *fall by the wayside,* we see that it could have been prevented if they had just turned to God. We mourn when we see children abused and people having sex irresponsibly, falling prey to drugs, crime, and perversion, as the words of God are ignored. We mourn when we see relatives and friends give up a life once committed to God, and become casualties of spiritual warfare. They leave families behind to chase after the shadows of happiness that seduced them in the world. We mourn when we think of how many are rejecting our creator, knowing that one day he will also reject them. We mourn when we think of how many men and women are locked away in jails, some giving up on life because of the hopelessness they feel. If you are reading this book and you are facing prison time, dedicate your life to the Most High God and watch as his transforming power change your circumstances. We also mourn because of the attacks we face ourselves, just because we are trying to live a life pleasing to God. As we mourn, let us remember the promise that we WILL be comforted. Every now and then God injects a ray of hope into our lives, letting us know that he still has us safe and secure in the palm of his hands. So let us live each day in expectation of the comfort that awaits us in eternity.

"Blessed are the meek: for they shall inherit the earth" (5:5).

Many people live convinced that they have to earn a certain amount of money to be happy, and put forth all of their effort at work with the dream of retiring. The hope money brings can be fulfilling, as you see the resources that it can provide for your family. However, people who only live to work do not truly enjoy life here on Earth. And when they do retire, they live in so much pain because of the damage they did to their bodies over the years. They rarely reap the full rewards of their labor. Yet many continue to live this way, especially in more developed countries. We should work hard. But in all of our work we must first seek to bring God honor and praise, never forgetting how tiny we are in relation to the whole of creation. And as we seek his will in all of our doings, we declare our meekness to him. We learn to rest in his grace, and take time out of our busy schedules to enjoy the simplicity of our families and our other resources. I must add here that it is the people who live on little, or who live each day as if it is the last day that they have with God, who find it easy to be meek in his presence. They move slower, and recognize the magnificent riches that our creator provided in nature. For them, it is a blessing just to breathe or to experience the rest of God's creation (nature). These are the blessed that will enjoy and inherit the bountiful riches of Earth.

"Blessed are they which do hunger and thirst after righteousness: for they shall be filled" (5:6).

Are you filled? I am not talking about being able to speak in tongues, as we are told is the only guarantee that someone is filled with the Spirit of God. Yes, some people do have this gift, but the fullness that Jesus talks about here is of God's powerful presence, which is his Spirit. When you hunger and thirst for righteousness you will seek God daily, asking him to teach you his ways. You will call out to him when you are in a crisis, and you will not stop praying until he answers you. You will diligently read his Word even when it is inconvenient to do so, and you will desperately ask him to give you a deeper understanding of his principles. You will seek him in all situations of your daily life. Then you will begin to feel it: the power of God's Holy Spirit moving all over you. The feeling is unmistakable, and the manifestations around you will change to reflect the power that is working in and through you. You will be so filled that everything you touch will reflect God's glory. Be careful though, for being filled does not always mean "loud". Sometimes being filled makes someone the most quiet one in the room. Watch out for the fruit which only the Spirit can bear, and you will know a lot about who is "filled"!

"Blessed are the merciful: for they shall obtain mercy" (5:7).

There is a common phrase that many of us know: "What goes around comes around." Similarly, when we choose to show kindness God blesses our lives with kindness. The kindness talked about here is not the one to gain a reward, or shown to those who can do something for us. This merciful kindness is shown to those who are hard to love or who are truly in need. Because of their lot in life, it is not normal for many to reach out to these people. When you pass a homeless person, do you just walk by with a kind word, or do you reach out and help him/ her in some meaningful way? When you know that someone is addicted to drugs, do you criticize them or do you fall on your knees and diligently pray for them- every day? When your children get in trouble, do you always give them the most severe punishment, or do you sometimes pardon them even though you are angry and hurt? When you see people sitting or standing by themselves, do you make an extra effort to speak with them, or do you turn away and pretend like they are not there? Reaching out a helping hand when you see a need, for no payment in return, is a show of mercy.

"Blessed are the pure in heart: for they shall see God" (5:8).

The pure in heart is not the person who always does everything *right*. Do you know of any such persons? The pure in heart seeks to love God with all of their heart, all of their mind, and all of their soul, and strives each day to love others as they love themselves. Everything that the "pure in heart" does is to honor the Most High God. You will know the pure in heart not just by the words they say, but by looking at their walk. How do these people treat others? How do these people show the love of God? The pure in heart will not always seem like the smartest or most outgoing one in the room. But their presence changes the atmosphere whenever and wherever they are present!

"Blessed are the peacemakers: for they shall be called the children of God" (5:9).

There are times when war is a part of God's divine order, but his main expectation for us is that we take the path of peace. We should not only say that we are peaceful, but we must practice being a peacemaker in all of our interactions. This being said, being a strife-maker and an instrument of gossip and division is not being a peacemaker. There will be times when, in spite of living peacefully, people in our lives will determine to make war with us.

We must seek God's guidance in how we should react. If you are in a place where you feel as though everyone wants to make war with you, stop. Instead of asking God what you should do, ask him to show you if the problem lies in you. Sometimes we are tempted with the thought that no one likes us, or that the world is out to get us and to rob us of our joy. God's law is in divine order and his will for his children, as noted in the verse above, is that we be a force of peace. Why would he tell us this, and set everyone in our lives against us? The only time this truly happens is when we are living in sin and our heavenly father wants to get our attention. In order to know if we are being tempted by forces of evil to keep our minds in bondage, or if our neighbors have been allowed to turn on us because we are in sin, ask God for guidance. He wants you his child to be an instrument of peace. If people around you are set on making war with you, do not run or hide. Make your presence felt, and let it be a presence of God's peace abiding in you. When he tells you to engage in spiritual warfare, it will always be according to his Word, and with the use of the sword, which is also his Word. Until such time, dwell confidently as a mighty warrior, raising the banner of God's peace.

"Blessed are they which are persecuted for righteousness' sake: for theirs is the kingdom of heaven" (5:10).

This message is not always taken well. While our society strongly values physical comfort, we are told here that part of living righteously is to experience discomfort. Being a follower of Jesus Christ causes us to be persecuted very often. Jesus rightfully prepares us by telling us here that we will be persecuted even for the sake of righteousness. We must not be naïve in thinking that our choice of letting God lead our lives, or our hope in eternal life, makes us immune from crisis. Any activity that glorifies the Most High puts us in the line of spiritual attack. All of a sudden *things* will happen around us to tempt us to feel discouraged and hopeless. We will be filled with joy in one moment, and tempted with a feeling of discouragement in another. We must determine to let God's Word inspire our peace and keep our hope alive!

Judge all thoughts that come to your mind and see if they line up with truth. Live and walk in the Spirit of God. This will not only arm you completely with his full armor, but will cause you to grow, thrive, and be fruitful in spite of persecution. Remember also that any blessing you receive now is but a shadow of what is to come in eternal life.

"Blessed are ye, when men shall revile you, and persecute you, and shall say all manner of evil against you falsely, for my sake" (5:11).

Being a follower of Jesus Christ comes with much ridicule, hate and accusations. Just as many thought that he was a rebel and a heretic while he lived on Earth, the same way we are labelled today by many. God is love, and created everything through his unconditional love. Knowing this, how could anyone who truly loves our heavenly father justify hating Jesus or anyone else? Yet people hate him and those who follow his teaching. So even though we prepare to live in peace, we must expect hate, ridicule and accusations. But we have a promise that even in these situations we will be blessed!

In verse thirteen Jesus sums up his teaching on humility by telling us that those who follow him are the 'salt of the earth'. We see with this declaration how essential humility is to being close to God. Jesus said, "Ye are the salt of the earth: but if the salt have lost his savour, wherewith shall it be salted? It is thenceforth good for nothing, but to be cast out, and to be trodden under foot of men" (Matthew 5:13). The emphasis on being the salt of the Earth at the end of his teaching on the mount tells me that humility is a vital part of being an 'unchained child of the Most High God'. This humility is not about our outward actions, or showing people around us what we can deprive ourselves of; it is about the inward dealings of each soul with our creator. It's about the conversations we have with God when no one else can hear us, and the conversations we have inwardly with ourselves when we think that he is not listening. Humility shows up in our thankfulness for the things placed in our lives. In our inner conversations, do we dream of all that WE can do in this world and the hereafter, or do we humbly worship our creator, and ask him to guide every step of our spiritual and physical lives?

The humility taught by Jesus is ultimately different from what the world teaches because he acknowledged his complete surrender to God and no one else. Jesus was very keen on directing all of his worship to the father. We are told:

"Ye are the light of the world. A city that is set on an hill cannot be hid. Neither do men light a candle, and put it under a bushel, but on a candlestick; and it giveth light unto all that are in the house. Let your light so shine before men, that they may see your good works, and glorify your Father which is in heaven" (5:14-16).

By this teaching, we see that when we are in perfect submission to God, we work in harmony with his plans, and in so doing we show the world examples of what he expects from all of his creation-perfect surrender to his will. This kind of humility and service to our creator is not easily accomplished but is a work in progress, and a daily choice. If humbling ourselves before the Most High was easy, he would not need to have candles (faithful believers), as everyone would create this light for themselves. The Holy Spirit is revealing to us that we are called to be outstanding, not to fit in! When we are humble and follow God completely, we shine his light by being a witness to the rest of the world.

Jesus' teachings on humility is also set apart from the world's version of humility because he told us that being in total surrender to God means following ALL of the principles of truth. Many religious people say that the laws of old were done away with by Jesus. But Jesus said, "Think not that I am come to destroy the law, or the prophets: I am not come to destroy, but to fulfill. For verily I say unto you, Till heaven and earth pass, one jot or one tittle shall in no wise pass from the law, till all be fulfilled" (Matthew 5:17-18). Let these words be etched into our minds. Jesus, having chosen the path of perfect obedience to our heavenly father, was able to clearly see the purpose of his life and do all the works that God expected him to do to its completion. In the same way, let us humbly seek God's will in every part of our lives.

Use this space to write about what you know about yourself. (Think of your likes, dislikes, strengths and weaknesses.)

Make a list of anything new that you have learned about our creator after reading this chapter on humility.

Ten

DIVINE LOVE

"Beloved, let us love one another: for love is of God; and every one that loveth is born of God, and knoweth God"

— (1 John 4:7).

The word "love" is one of the most widely used words that we have today. But what we think of as love is far different from the true love of God. Even though love is talked about so frequently, many are left at the end of the day asking, "What is love?" The divine love of God is true love because God IS love! Anything else that professes itself to be love is limited and based on our human understanding. We cannot fully capture the total essence of the love of God- which many religious scholars call *Agape* love. And many people have turned away from our creator because they blame him for the horrors of this world. In this chapter, some of the answers to the questions we have about love will be given. And as we study the love of God, we will see the deeper meaning behind some of the problems we face.

Why does God allow bad things to happen? He sometimes allows things to happen in our lives to draw us back to him. You see, the fallen state of our existence can be rectified when in our challenges we learn to call out to him. Whatever situations he thinks is best to bring us completely back to him is what he will allow in our lives. For example, the people of Israel were not chosen because God hated other groups, as some people may think. One reason why the nation of Israel was chosen is because God found members of that blood line to be righteous beyond reproof. He therefore blessed an entire group of people because of the influence he knew these righteous men and women will have on, not just Israel, but the rest of the world. Next, the descendants of Israel were chosen to be God's witnesses of his divine love because of their deep desire to get to know him on a personal level. He has used them time and again to show the rest of mankind what happens when we obey his divine laws and what happens when we choose to reject his love. Thirdly, the Israelites represent the whole of humanity and show us how fickle we are and how easy it is for us to reject our heavenly father.

That being said, he never punishes anyone because he is a wicked, perverted creator. His laws are always clearly revealed to us, and it is by our choices that we keep or break them, creating the consequences that we have. There are consequences for our thoughts, words and actions. God inevitably controls it all, but he still gives us freewill to choose whether or not we will obey him. We cannot fully understand how all of it fits together because we are not the creator. Which student of one class can say that he understands everything about his entire school? In the same respect, our only job is to correctly interpret the particular lesson that God has us in in the present moment. And which student promotes or fails herself after taking a test? In the saga of the Israelites in the book of Joshua, they were given clear directions of what was expected from them, and the consequences were laid out. Just as God promised, when the Israelites obeyed, they lived in peace with their neighbors; and when they lived in disobedience they were at war with all of their neighbors.

We see from this that we cause our own calamity because of what is seen in our hearts. Our creator has messengers and spiritual workers behind the scenes, working out the situations that we bring upon ourselves. He places key experiences and people in our lives at specific times to bring about transformation and cause us to be in harmony with him. To what extent do we have free range under God's control? Only he knows this answer. When Almighty God first created us, he knew what would be found in each soul, and he designed specific situations for each of his children to return to him. But at the end of the day, the choice is ours. This choice is made at a level which we cannot inspect in each other, or even in ourselves sometimes. But God, who created our souls, knows how to inspect us and assess the quality and development of our love. We must come to the point where we truly love serving and obeying him, not because of the consequences, but because of our faith in his love for us.

What we see around us in our physical lives is a mere shadow. And as the wisest man, Solomon, said, "I have seen all the works that are done under the sun; and, behold, all is vanity and vexation of spirit" (Ecclesiastes 1:14). I am not saying that the things around us don't exist, or that we are not supposed to enjoy them. They do exist, and we should enjoy them if doing so pleases God, but at the end of the day, the only thing that matters is our soul's growth in the divine love of the Most High God.

It is in our souls that we choose to be in or out of harmony with God. The real you and the real me is found in our soul, and this is what God has always worked on so that he can save us and bring us back into a harmonious relationship with him. We were not created to see life in terms of good and evil but in terms of obedience to his every command. But we brought about the reality of *good and evil* by our disobedience. No matter how terrible our circumstances are, we must first know that our creator has our best interest at heart. Then we must admit to two things: that without God we are weak and can only overcome challenges through him, and that we may be in the wrong and not know it sometimes. We must then ask him to show us his will for that situation. If we sincerely ask, and we are truly humbled to know God's will for our lives, he will reveal the answers and show us exactly what needs to be done. This then further builds his trust in us, and he draws closer to us, even as we draw closer to him. Each individual soul has a unique set of lessons to be learned in this life and each day has been uniquely designed to achieve this learning. Many of us fail and don't learn at the pace that God wants us to learn because we choose to be stubborn and wrestle with him.

It is therefore very important that even as we learn we also teach our children about the love of God. We must show them this love through stories found in his Word, and also by the example of how we live our daily lives. How do we treat our spouses in the home? Do we tell our children that we love them? Do we let our spouse win some arguments, or do we insist on always getting our own way? Do we sometimes spend time talking with our children without the interruption of devices and work? These questions must provoke us to action and guide us in how we show the love of God in our homes.

This is important because our children are being bombarded with various choices in lifestyles at a very early age. This bombardment affects the role of the parents as the first teachers. Did you know that by age five, a child has already made solid conclusions about life in his/her mind that is very difficult to change after that? You may have sent your children out to childcare since they were babies, thinking that it is the teacher's responsibility to teach your child. But know this: a parent is a child's first teacher. Children glean most of their learning from the home then go to school to practice what they learn. So if you have not been teaching your child at home because you thought it was the teacher's job, please change that mindset right now and follow the steps given here. Many children are rebellious at school because they do not have a solid respect for their parents based on a love that was to be established by the time they turned five. If work is never done to correct this relationship between parent(s) and child, or that growing person does not come to have a personal relationship with God through Christ, that individual grows up to be a rebellious adult in society.

When Jesus was asked by his disciples which is the greatest commandment, he answered:

> Thou shalt love the Lord thy God with all thy heart, and with all thy soul, and with all thy mind. This is the first and great commandment. And the second is like unto it, Thou shalt love thy neighbour as thyself. On these two commandments hang all the law and the prophets (Matthew 22:36-40).

Notice two things about these two commandments: they are both centered around love, and every other commandment or all other principles of the Word of God rest on them. If you want to teach your children and do not know where to begin, start here with these two commandments revealed by Jesus Christ. When we come to a place where in our fight with God we choose not to let go, but to hold on tight with the determination to know him more and more, he sees us as worthy and reveals more of himself to us. We fall deeper in love with him, and the choice to obey his will for our lives becomes an easier one to make.

Who are some people in your life that are difficult to love?

What aspect about yourself in the past was difficult to love?

What are some things in your life that you can be thankful for?

Spend five minutes or more with each of your children, in private from the others and tell them this:

"..............I love you very much. I will ask God to help me do my very best to raise you. From today I promise to spend more time with you, to be consistent, and to listen to your concerns.
If you follow our rules and obey God, you will be rewarded. But if you do not follow the rules of our home, or disobey God, there will be consequences"

Later on that week, have a family meeting with all of the children and take about an hour, creating rules, rewards and consequences for the family. Encourage everyone to be practical with their ideas. Create a chart As soon as you can, make copies and hang them in key areas in the home. Finally, make sure the family is consistent in following the plan made. The plan that was created can be changed each year, or as your family changes.

There is an additional method that we use in our home to develop a better relationship with our children. Each week, or at least once a month, we have a "time out" with each child. This is not the time out where you let the child spend time alone as a form of punishment. My uncle, who vacationed with my family one year, taught me this method. With this "Time Out", spend time alone with each child, finding out from them if they have any concerns in their personal lives, or if they have suggestions on how you can improve as a parent Take time to listen. Be patient, and come up with realistic ways that their concerns can be worked out

Eleven

DIVINE HARMONY

For as the body is one, and hath many members, and all the members of that one body, being many, are one body: so also is Christ. For by one Spirit are we all baptized into one body, whether we be Jews or Gentiles, whether we be bond or free; and have been all made to drink into one Spirit. For the body is not one member, but many. If the foot shall say, Because I am not the hand, I am not of the body; is it therefore not of the body? And if the ear shall say, Because I am not the eye, I am not of the body; is it therefore not of the body? If the whole body were an eye, where were the hearing? If the whole were hearing, where were the smelling? But now hath God set the members every one of them in the body, as it hath pleased him. And if they were all one member, where were the body? But now are they many members, yet but one body. And the eye cannot say unto the hand, I have no need of thee: nor again the head to the feet, I have no need of you. Nay, much more those members of the body, which seem to be more feeble, are necessary: And those members of the body, which we think to be less honourable, upon these we bestow more abundant honour; and our uncomely parts have more abundant comeliness. For our comely parts have no need: but God hath tempered the body together, having given more abundant honour to that part which lacked: That there should be no schism in the body; but that the members should have the same care one for another. And whether one member suffer, all the members suffer with it; or one member be honoured, all the members rejoice with it

— (1 CORINTHIANS 12:12-26).

62

*T*ake a few minutes to look at yourself in the mirror. You will see something that is simply amazing: harmony. It is not the harmony that the world tells us we can achieve if we just believe in the goodness of man. We are talking here about the harmony that already exists in the entire creation from the tiniest of atoms, to the complex network of heavenly bodies above us. This is the harmony that you were created with. The trees breathe out oxygen which we need to breathe in in order to live; and we breathe out Carbon dioxide which the plants need in order to live. Each breath we take keeps our bodies alive moment by moment, and our heart is able to pump air and blood to every tiny crease of our bodies. All of this happens without our control, kept in perfect harmony and timing by the one who created us. Everything in nature is perfectly synchronized in the same way as our bodies. Yet many of us go about life ignoring this magnificent gift of life and the many creations in nature given to us to enjoy. If we are to come into the perfect will of God, we must recognize that the body that each of us is given is a perfect and powerful vehicle, created by him and for him. Secondly, we need to accept that our bodies were created to function in harmony with the rest of his creation. Whether or not we choose to believe in God's divine harmony, it is truth, and our bodies, along with the rest of the universe, testify of a harmonious relationship. That is why the nutrients and vitamins from the foods we eat know exactly which part of our body to travel to and work on. Even the plants that we use as food and medicine are naturally color coded to match the various organs of our bodies.

As we take a closer look at the genius of the human body, it clearly reveals the design of an intelligent and wonderful creator. Yet we find reasons to not believe in creation. Did you make yourself? Where did your body come from? Each day of life we experience the miracle of breathing. We might be able to make ourselves breathe slower or faster, but what controls our breathing when we are not even paying attention to it? As you breathe right now, think about what would happen if you should hold your breath and stop inhaling, disrupting the flow of harmony. Have you ever wondered how we are able to breathe in and out and how the body is able to use the gases that are breathed in to fuel the other organs within it? The way our body functions should be enough to give us a healthy fear and respect of God, who intelligently keeps everything together and in its right place. The human body, like the rest of nature, functions in perfect harmony until we tamper with our creator's genius with products that are not in harmony with the law of creation. Then when nature reacts and we are plagued by disease, we blame God.

Earth and the many other celestial bodies in the universe display the same harmony as within our bodies. Each day we observe the phases of the moon and the life giving power of the sun. We study their cycles. We use this information as guides for our signs and seasons. Yet many do not even realize that it is by careful study of these heavenly creations that farmers plant their crops to feed us. Also most, if not all, animals are born based on the phases of the moon. Our weather, the seasons, and the tides of the seas are also influenced by the moon. Yet we go about life in much ignorance about the influence of these creations. And when some people discover their significance, they worship these created beings instead of seeking to worship the one who created them. Even the trees do what God created them to do. When the air gets cold they hibernate, and as the air warms up again these same trees reawaken. These cycles happen at specific times and show not chaos and confusion, but harmony. Who teaches the roosters to crow at sunrise? Look around at nature and you will see countless harmonious relationships and the genius of an intelligent creator. Who taught the animals to come out in the spring? And who taught them to prepare their homes and store meals for the colder seasons?

Many readers will say that the answer to these questions is evolution; that these animals just learned to survive over millions of years. However, I will leave these points with you: First, evolution is a theory, meaning a guess. It is therefore as good a guess as any other guesses. Secondly, in the theory of evolution man is the most highly evolved creature. If we are so evolved why is it that the more advanced our society is, the more we go against nature? Why do we struggle to understand some basic things that tiny animals know? The more "developed" we are, the more we neglect the harmonious relationships in nature, while all the other created beings function in perfect harmony! All of the animals and plants know how to survive in harsh situations; they train their young better than we train ours, and in many cases it is we who need them to survive and not the other way around.

Our creator tells us to observe the animals; even the tiny ant we are to learn from (Proverbs 6:6-7). The Most High shows us time and again that every one of his creations was designed to work together in harmony. Disturb one aspect of nature and the entire environment is affected. It is therefore a necessity that we stay focused on staying in God's will, which will put us in perfect harmony. As I continue to stress, this determination to let God lead your life is an internal, personal choice, and will not always be recognized at first glance. Therefore, in striving to remain in his perfect will we must watch how we interpret situations and people, and try at all cost not to judge others. Instead, in every situation we find ourselves in, we must ask God, "How should I interpret and respond to this?"

We see from all of these examples that harmony is natural and it is only by deliberate choice that a person refuses to be in harmony with God's plans. When in our minds we choose to function outside of his will, we take ourselves out of divine harmony, and even though it might seem as if we are successful, we actually die little by little on the inside. We become disconnected like a fruit that is picked from a tree, and our soul stops growing. The sign that this growth has stopped is the stagnation that you feel on the inside, and the hypocrite that you look like on the outside. The Bible tells us that we will know those whose hearts are in obedience to God by their fruit (Matthew 7:15-20). The writer also tells us that people will be professing to bare the fruit of God's Spirit and will do many forms of miracles and wonders. These physical acts might seem convincing, but the fruit of the Spirit is love, joy, peace, longsuffering, gentleness, goodness, faith, meekness, and temperance (Galations 5:22-23). Again, when judging fruit, we must look at the person's spiritual life and not their physical.

What part does evil play in God's divine harmony? Our creator knew what would happen when man encountered Satan and yet he orchestrated everything to work in perfect harmony. He did not want man to have the knowledge of 'good and evil' in the beginning, but he saw even then that through our difficult circumstances we will learn to depend on him and understand the depths of his love. The difficulties and the pain that we experience should not simply be identified as 'good or evil'. We must also be conscious of the influence that the forces of unrighteousness have among us. The good news is that if we repent and totally dedicate our lives to God, he can turn any situation around in our favor and bring us back to his initial plan of perfection. When we look at life this way, we see the whole picture in terms of divine order instead of 'good versus evil'. And we take the focus off of the enemy and place all of our concentration on what our creator wants to do in our lives. Did God know that Adam and Eve would fall prey to Satan? His word tells us so. "Then hear thou in heaven thy dwelling place, and forgive, and do, and give to every man according to his ways, whose heart thou knowest; (for thou, even thou only, knowest the hearts of all the children of men)" (1 Kings 8:39). This shows us that it is in man's heart (emotional center) where sin is born and the passage also lets us know that our creator knows all the generations that will ever exist.

This idea that we have a part to play in our own destiny with the choices we make is clearly summed up in the passage of Proverbs, which reads, "A man's heart deviseth his way: but the LORD directeth his steps" (Proverbs 16:9). How is it then that God is all knowing, and is in control of our destiny, but we are still given the freedom to choose? He shows us through this verse that in our hearts we make choices of whether to obey or disobey, and when God sees our choices, he rewards us accordingly and plans our circumstances to match those choices of our hearts. His desire, though, is for all of us to choose to love and obey him. Even though man chooses in his mind of whether he will obey or disobey, God invests a lot into teaching us how to make "right" choices. He does this by showing us again and again, through scripture and our daily experiences, what choices and thoughts we must entertain and what thoughts we should reject.

I cannot say that I know how long the arm of God's control is and to what extent he gives us control over our own physical lives. But what I do know is that at the end of the day everything works in total harmony.

In learning about divine harmony, it is natural for us to ask how Satan fits in if he is allowed to disobey God. God created Satan for a perfect purpose as part of his master plan, but Satan chose within himself to believe that he could have an existence outside of God's law. This is what we learn about Satan from the book of John: "He was a murderer from the beginning, and abode not in the truth, because there is no truth in him. When he speaketh a lie, he speaketh of his own: for he is a liar, and the father of it" (John 8:44). We see from this that Satan invented sin: the lie that there is an existence outside of God's plan. God knew what would happen when man encountered Satan, so he prepared a way out for all of us! The way he prepared was through the life, death and resurrection of Jesus Christ. His main purpose for his children today is to make us like Christ, the way he initially intended when he first conceived us. The choice to believe like Satan believed is disharmony and sin. The choice to obey God and follow the way of Jesus puts us in divine harmony with God. Which will you choose?

What caused Satan to sin? The short answer is pride. His amazing beauty and his phenomenal powers caused him to feel like he could be apart from God's will, and he desired to have his own way. He lied when in pride he thought that he could be the creator also, and not simply 'the created'. Please feel free to look up the scriptural references below to reinforce this truth that God saw everything he made as good and in perfect harmony (Colossians 1:16, John 1:3, Romans 11:36). God expected man to view his existence and the rest of creation in this way of complete perfection, and it was Satan's work that showed Adam and Eve this knowledge of 'good and evil'. It was not just the tree that caused Adam and Eve's downfall. It was also the thought that was entertained that somehow they could do as they wanted and disobey God that caused their and our downfall. God told Adam the final consequence of what would happen if that fruit was eaten, while Satan only told Eve of the initial consequence. We must recognize the skillful craft of our enemy, Satan, who through his many employees, continue to twist the truth, thereby making a fool out of us and stealing the birthright from those who will listen to him. For those who still continue to think that our creator is petty and love to see us die, I have a question for you: Why would God form us with such precision and create everything so beautiful and harmonious, just to taunt, tempt, and torture us?

There is no mistake then in God because he sees everything as a whole, while our minds perceive life based on our debilitating inheritance of sin. He sees how it all can work together in his divine order. One day we will be united with the creator in perfect harmony. And at that time, we will remember our lives here on Earth and see that every experience served to bring us back to him and not to tempt us to draw further away from him. The difficult circumstances that sin causes can actually draw us closer to God if we run to him. Not wanting to deal with these consequences of sin, we will strive to stay on the path of righteousness. This is in essence what God meant when he forbade Adam and Eve to eat from the tree of good and evil. You might then ask: Why did he put the tree in the garden? The answer is that he already knew what was in their hearts and how they would be deceived. As a result, he put that tree in the middle of the garden so that no one could accuse him of not making the tree visible enough, or not giving Adam and Eve sufficient warning. He sees the present, the past, and the future, and all of these are one because he is not bound by time or space. Our creator is like a film director who has already captured a scene for a movie, and can decide whether or not to let the characters do a retake to change certain parts of it. God has provided a bypass for us to get what he intends for us to get at his perfect timing. Let us now consider the passage below from the book of Ephesians which explains his sovereignty perfectly!

> Blessed be the God and Father of our Lord Jesus Christ, who hath blessed us with all spiritual blessings in heavenly places in Christ: According as he hath chosen us in him before the foundation of the world, that we should be holy and without blame before him in love: Having predestinated us unto the adoption of children by Jesus Christ to himself, according to the good pleasure of his will, To the praise of the glory of his grace, wherein he hath made us accepted in the beloved. In whom we have redemption through his blood, the forgiveness of sins, according to the riches of his grace; Wherein he hath abounded toward us in all wisdom and prudence; Having made known unto us the mystery of his will, according to his good pleasure which he hath purposed in himself: That in the dispensation of the fullness of times he might gather together in one all things in Christ, both which are in heaven, and which are on earth; even in him: In whom also we have obtained an inheritance, being predestinated according to the purpose of him who worketh all things after the counsel of his own will (Ephesians 1:3-11).

From this passage of scripture, we see that God knew from before he created us who will choose the path of Christ (a soul humbled in total obedience to him) and who will choose the path of Satan (a prideful soul in disobedience to God's harmonious law). If it wasn't for the souls that will choose the path of obedience, God would have already destroyed everything on Earth and start over, just like he did in times past. He gives everyone an equal opportunity to hear truth, so that each person can make an individual choice to obey him. Satan does his job of discrediting our creator every chance he gets, like a rebellious child would. But God makes sure that in every age, there are witnesses, his candles, to light the way for those who will turn to him. He puts the facts directly in front of us, like the forbidden tree that he placed in the middle of Eden. And he uses other examples, like the children of Israel, to show us that even though he is long suffering, there are consequences for our choices. The elements around us in nature testify that God is real. What will it take for you to believe?

Spend some time in nature today or as soon as possible for ten minutes or more. As you interact with God's creation, take note of the harmony that you observe.

Look at yourself in the mirror. What parts of your body do you love and why?

What parts of your body don't you love and why?

Gillian Herman-Davis

What would it take for you to see your body as perfect? Be honest.

Spend some time in deeper study and meditation of the passage of scripture below.

I will praise thee; for I am fearfully and wonderfully made: marvellous are thy works; and that my soul knoweth right well. My substance was not hid from thee, when I was made in secret, and curiously wrought in the lowest parts of the earth. Thine eyes did see my substance, yet being unperfect; and in thy book all my members were written, which in continuance were fashioned, when as yet there was none of them. How precious also are thy thoughts unto me, O God! how great is the sum of them! (Psalm 139:14-17)

Now ask God to teach you how to love and value each part of your body.

Take note of what he says.

Twelve

DIVINE CONSEQUENCE

"But the fruit of the Spirit is love, joy, peace, longsuffering, gentleness, goodness, faith, Meekness, temperance: against such there is no law"
— (GALATIONS 5:22-23).

As we dedicate our lives to God, we must understand that all were created to obey the law of consequence or cause and effect and that there are consequences for each and every choice that we make. God knows the power of our choices and that is why he tells us over and over again that we need to focus on thoughts of righteousness which no law can come against (Galations 5:22-23). These thoughts place us in harmony with the rest of creation and keep us safe and secure in his will.

The world tells us that there is good in all, and that if we seek out the goodness in all men, we can have a perfect world as in the Garden of Eden. This idea of a utopian society is not new with God, as he tells us in his word that this is how he initially intended for us to live. But man's choices in Eden to disobey created the consequences of disharmony that we have now. We therefore cannot rely on mankind to save us. Through the knowledge of God's law, we must help each other to put our focus back on following him, and accept his saving grace through Jesus Christ. Adam and Eve ate of the forbidden tree of the knowledge of good and evil and that caused each of us to experience a fallen state. So how can *our* good save us? Rather, we must help one another to repent and return to total obedience of God through the way of Jesus Christ.

All that God created he called "good", and there is goodness in all men because God's breath is in all of us. However, we all inherited the consequences of sin because of Adam and Eve's disobedience, and in our weakened state we are all prey to the spiritual wickedness around us which we fight every day. So no matter how much we believe in the goodness of man, people among us will be influenced to lie, steal, kill, fornicate, commit adultery, be prideful, and do many other things that are against God's law. These experiences are the effects of our spiritual separation from God. But we can turn back to him if we recognize our need to return to the original image which he had for us in the beginning.

We each must choose the path of salvation in order for our reconciliation with our creator to happen. Will we choose the path of total obedience or will we continue to let sin control our lives? Choosing to be reconciled back with God does not stop with this decision. Our entire lives must be committed to following the way of Jesus Christ. This complete surrender to God's will must become our new lifestyle as we realize that the consequences of every action have far reaching effects. If we do not see this from Adam and Eve's simple choice of eating a forbidden fruit, I don't know what will show us. To allow the Holy Spirit to have full control over our lives, we must have faith; all of the hopes and dreams that we have for our lives must come second to what God wants. This is complete surrender, not because he is a petty creator who only wants to punish us, but because he is our father who loves us and wants the best for us.

He knows us, and just like with the rest of creation, he knows that our actions bring on certain consequences. Our heavenly father knows that when we rely on our own understanding, we will fall into the same snare that Adam and Eve fell into. Exchanging our lusts or desires for God's desires will cause us to be in total harmony with his perfect law of consequence. His Word shows us that he has made us for a special purpose which we cannot fully understand at this time (1 Corinthians 2:9). To show how special we are to him, it is written, "Of his own will begat he us with the word of truth, that we should be a kind of first fruits of his creatures" (James 1:18). Even though we don't fully understand what it means to be *firstfruits* of God, we get a clear sense that he is preparing us to be a showpiece in all of his creation.

God created us for a special purpose if scripture calls us the "first fruits" of his other creations. We have to stop accepting the lies that we believed to be true for all these years. There is a hell, and there will be a day when those who remain in disobedience to God's laws will face the ultimate penalty for their choices. Knowing this, we must become more watchful of our thoughts, words and actions, because everything that we do has a direct or indirect consequence on what God will allow next into our lives. I believe that when we are told to do unto others as we would have others do to us, it is a warning that we must be more aware of the far reaching consequences of our thoughts and actions. Scripture tells us over and over again to entertain pure thoughts. "Finally, brethren, whatsoever things are true, whatsoever things are honest, whatsoever things are just, whatsoever things are pure, whatsoever things are lovely, whatsoever things are of good report; if there be any virtue, and if there be any praise, think on these things" (Philippians 4:8). Focusing on these attributes keeps our souls in the right place when we encounter spiritual warfare, and causes us to escape without irreparable harm to our souls.

There is a story in the book of Matthew that also tells of God's divine principle of consequence (cause and effect).

Another parable put he forth unto them, saying, The kingdom of heaven is likened unto a man which sowed good seed in his field: But while men slept, his enemy came and sowed tares among the wheat, and went his way. But when the blade was sprung up, and brought forth fruit, then appeared the tares also. So the servants of the householder came and said unto him, Sir, didst not thou sow good seed in thy field? From whence then hath it tares? He said unto them, An enemy hath done this. The servants said unto him, Wilt thou then that we go and gather them up? But he said, Nay; lest while ye gather up the tares, ye root up also the wheat with them. Let both grow together until the harvest: and in the time of harvest I will say to the reapers, Gather ye together first the tares, and bind them in bundles to burn them: but gather the wheat into my barn (Matthew 13:24-30).

Let us now consider this analogy of the kingdom of heaven. God allowed his seed and the evil one's tares (sin) to grow together because of the devastating effect that would arise from him pulling the tares out prematurely. There could be a family of five: two members could choose to live a life of obedience to God while three could choose to reject him. The father of these children may have not chosen the way of obedience to God. Now what if our heavenly father had NOT allowed this father to live out his full years? Then his children would not have been born and given the opportunity to choose. Our creator knows each one of his children, and he also knew from the beginning that because of sin only some of us would choose to be reconciled back to him. So he allows the full completion of time to occur so that all souls will be given the opportunity to live and to choose. Therefore, the kingdom of heaven continues until time is fulfilled and every soul that God has conceived is given their fair chance. Even though we might not grasp all that God has done or will do, know that he is good and he is in control all the time. He has an intelligent, divine reason for all of his actions and his divine law does not depend on our understanding of it!

Whatever we need to work on in our souls will affect what God allows to enter our lives. When these situations come, we respond based on our soul's level of growth. His goal for every believer is for us to grow closer to him and exercise mature faith in spite of difficult circumstances. If we experience people constantly doubting us, it might be because God saw that our soul has the tendency to accept quick defeat. Therefore he will continually allow this into our lives until we become skillful at standing strong on our faith in him. He will allow us to go through this training until we learn to say, "I know I can win in this situation because of the power of God in me. So in spite of what I see, I will not lose hope." Have you ever noticed that when you feel a certain way about a person or a situation, the more things seem to happen to prove that you are right? Think about the famous children's story about the train, which when it believed that it could, it did. The moral of that story is: "If you think you can, you will. And if you think you can't, you won't". God's divine principle of consequence works somewhat the same in our lives. And so he does not make a mistake when he tells us to align our thoughts with the righteous attributes of his Spirit. God knows that by doing this our lives will manifest the fruit of his Spirit, and the effects will be liberating and for our best interest.

If you feel like you do not have, you will continue to not have in your own mind. Even though you will possess many assets, you'll continue to have thoughts of fear, poverty and lack. Deep inside, you will not want to share what you have for fear of running out of resources. This is described in the book of Proverbs and we are told that as a man thinks in his heart so is he (Proverbs 23:7). Any transformation must start from within. We must ask God to transform our thoughts and emotions to the positive traits he calls the fruit of the Spirit. The change within our thoughts and emotions will then affect our mind, causing us to surrender our will to his will. Our thoughts will thus change based on our new humbled will, and our emotions will be controlled instead of our emotions controlling our mind. This cycle will continue in perfect harmony, the way it was meant to be, and it will open the floodgates of heaven as the Spirit of God will establish full reign in our lives. This will, in effect, change the way we respond to the people and experiences which God allows into our lives. We are appropriately told in the Word that all things work together for good, for them that love God and are called according to his purpose (Romans 8:27-29). In recognizing that everything we think, say or do has consequences, let us understand the importance of prayer. Let us stop for a moment and ask our heavenly father to help us get back into his will for our lives and teach us how to remain in his will forevermore.

Heavenly father, I give you my heart, my mind and my soul. Please teach me how to forgive the people who I feel have offended me. Show me what is in my heart today, and help me to be obedient to you. Show me how to react to situations I find myself in. Help me to patiently experience everything that you want me to experience. Guide me to see your will in every situation and in every encounter. Direct my thoughts, control the reigns of my emotions and let my will be in harmony with your will. Teach me the power of the life, death and resurrection of Jesus Christ and help me to be victorious and not a victim of sin. Amen.

What have you learned so far about our creator?

Part Two

Who Am I?

"Ask, and it shall be given you; seek, and ye shall find; knock, and it shall be opened unto you: For every one that asketh receiveth; and he that seeketh findeth; and to him that knocketh it shall be opened. Or what man is there of you, whom if his son ask bread, will he give him a stone? Or if he ask a fish, will he give him a serpent? If ye then, being evil, know how to give good gifts unto your children, how much more shall your Father which is in heaven give good things to them that ask him? (Matthew 7:7-11).

Thirteen

Operation S and F

And as for thy nativity, in the day thou wast born thy navel was not cut, neither wast thou washed in water to supple thee; thou wast not salted at all, nor swaddled at all. None eye pitied thee, to do any of these unto thee, to have compassion upon thee; but thou wast cast out in the open field, to the lothing of thy person, in the day that thou wast born. And when I passed by thee, and saw thee polluted in thine own blood, I said unto thee when thou wast in thy blood, Live; yea, I said unto thee when thou wast in thy blood, Live. I have caused thee to multiply as the bud of the field, and thou hast increased and waxen great, and thou art come to excellent ornaments: thy breasts are fashioned, and thine hair is grown, whereas thou wast naked and bare. Now when I passed by thee, and looked upon thee, behold, thy time was the time of love; and I spread my skirt over thee, and covered thy nakedness: yea, I sware unto thee, and entered into a covenant with thee, saith the Lord GOD, and thou becamest mine

— (EZEKIEL 16:4-8).

There is not one word that completely describes who we are because we were made in the image and likeness of the Most High God, and he cannot be described by just one word.

We spend our entire lives looking for one word that could tell who we are, but we will never find it. We are not a color either. Many of us identify ourselves and others based a color, when this is a figment of our imagination that raises itself above the words of God; one's color is the furthest thing from the truth. We are not our bodies, but souls in bodies; therefore the color of our skin does not make us who we are. We are each a combination of traits which God determined from before our time began.

As you study the next few chapters in section two, do not look for one word that fully captures the essence of who you are. Rather, look for the many qualities that God says you have. Know that you will never be able to know everything about who you truly are, because you did not create yourself. Only God knows who you are and who he would like to transform you to be. You may think that you are a finished product, having been created in his image. But we are all a work in progress, and God is not finished with us yet. He sees us as his great treasure that in time will be fully refined- diamonds in the rough!

Even though this chapter's opening scripture refers to the Israelites, it gives a heart-wrenching image of how we are when God begins his work on us. Time and time again the people of Israel fall away from God and sink into further disaster. But every time they turn back to him, he wraps his love around them, cleans them up and prepares them to stand once again in glory. Just like the Israelites, we are all God's children. He wants to give each of us an identity in him, but first he must cleanse and redeem us to the full glory which we had when he first conceived us. Like Israel, we stubbornly pull our hands away from his, in ignorance of who he is and who we are. We prefer to remain in the filth of ignorance and temporary pleasure. We refuse to open our eyes and see the glory of our creator and what he is trying to do through us.

The Most High finds each of his children in the terrible mess of our sins. When we choose to surrender our lives completely to him he begins the process of cleansing and renewal within our souls, which we call sanctification. Throughout the process of our sanctification, he places specific people in our lives at specific times to work on us as he sees fit, and it is this interaction between God's people that we generally refer to as *fellowship*. This chapter is titled: 'Operation S and F' because it is about seeing the connection between the process of sanctification and the tool of fellowship.

The remainder of this chapter is written in the form of a letter because it is a more personal approach for a very personal subject matter, and I hope that it has the effect on you that God wants it to have.

- The word "neighbor" in this context is anyone who we interact with in our life, whether it's a friend, family member, co-worker, teammate, opponent, or member of any other group we belong to.

Dear Reader,

As you read this letter, please have an open mind and ask God to clearly reveal to you what he would like you to learn. Then determine that you will apply all that you learn.

You may be in either of three experiences right now: you may have just come out of a conflict with one of your neighbors, you might be in a conflict right now with one or more of your neighbors; or you are about to enter into a conflict with one or more of your neighbors. This is because sin has made the operations of conflict to be a constant in our lives, and it is through these conflicts that our creator must teach us vital lessons in order to draw us back to him. A friend of mine once said, "There are sinners on the road- conflict, sinners at church- conflict, sinners in the home- conflict. We are all sinners, saved by God's grace, and because we are all sinners, conflict is inevitable!" With conflict you and I are shown what needs to be further cleansed from our own lives and from the lives of our neighbors. Conflicts also show us what have already been sanctified (perfected) in our lives, and reveals what else needs more work. All of this happens as we interact day to day with the people who God places in our lives.

We even experience conflict in our own minds sometimes because we don't realize that there is a divine purpose for the difficulties that come into our lives. I used to be a *people pleaser*. As God started to rip this cancer out of my life, I got annoyed when the people I wanted so bad to please found fault with me. I didn't realize that this was his way of removing that impurity from my life, so I held on tight with everything I had. It was all I knew how to do. As you can imagine, there was great conflict within me because no matter how hard I tried, I just could not get people to see me the way I tried to present myself. When God finally got my attention, I was strung out with self-pity, resentment and bitterness. I was filled with pride as well because I thought that I didn't deserve the way I was treated. The Most High showed me that I first had to come to a place where I faced my own sins. This was the only way that he could continue the process of my healing.

When God puts you in a place to face your sins it is very difficult because you feel as though you are losing your identity and the things that mostly make you who you are. I was in a dilemma. The more I thought that it was other people's fault, the more I remained in my custom-made puddle of grief. I became stagnant in every way. I didn't know that this was because I would not face the worse things about myself. But when I finally faced my flaws, I realized how low I had sunk and how much I depended on other people's validation.

I asked God to help me and he did. He showed me that I was treating myself and other people as idols, and that I needed to remove those barriers so that he could continue my process of sanctification. It took me years to grasp this lesson because I thought that I was a righteous person, not capable of idolizing anyone. Now that I am free from 'people worship', I am ready to expose my life to the world, and openly declare the grace and mercies of God without fear of criticism.

Since God opened my eyes to this truth, I have become more careful each day in making sure that my goal is not to please others but to please him. Now I pray for other people more than I try to gain their approval. In the past, I stayed up many nights going over conversations that I've had the day before, picking each line apart, wondering if I might have offended someone. Now I do not speak until I know for sure that it is God's will for me to open my mouth. No matter what situation I am in, I keep quiet until it is essential to speak, instead of rambling just for the sake of pleasing someone. And when I speak, I do so responsibly and with sincerity, without fear of ridicule. I know that God will never tell me to do something corrupt or against his principles and I am no longer plagued by the anxiety to keep everyone around me happy. I see the confusion on people's faces sometimes as they wonder why I am not responding the way I usually did before.

This brings me to my second reason for why we get into conflicts. We sometimes get into conflict because we are ignorant about what God has done or is doing in someone else's life. We judge our neighbors before asking him for guidance. We think that because people don't do the things we do, speak the way we speak, or think the way we think, we are in a 'better place' than they are. We do all manner of things to get them to act in the frame that we think they fit in. But this is destructive and must be stopped. We are all sinners because of our inherited sin nature. As a result of sin, we have all fallen from the position that God initially planned for us. As a result of our fallen state, our eyes are blurred, our emotions have been corrupted, and our thoughts have been hijacked. We are not able to see the perfect will of God in our lives and in the lives of others. Our creator tries every day to undo this corruption and to teach us to see people the way he sees them. He allows us to be in situations where we have to see and act through unconditional love.

We need to realize that we are all on this spiritual journey to-
gether and need each other to catch us when we fall. It is when we
learn to see like God sees that he will remove that particular con-
flict, or that particular personality type, from our lives. And when
this happens, we are a step purer in his process of sanctification.

God sanctifies us by giving us conflicts in which we have to learn
to forgive. Forgiveness is based on the divine love of God because it
takes unconditional love to perform this ongoing action. Our heav-
enly father wants us to be sanctified to the point where we love like
he does all the time. When your neighbor does, says or thinks some-
thing that you do not like, do you pull into your own self-righteous-
ness, in which you immediately say to yourself, "I would never do
that, God help them"? We have all done this at some point. But the
only way that God can continue his work of cleaning you up is when
you take the time to acknowledge your own sin. This involves taking
the time and having the courage to look inward, and say, "God show
me where I am in the wrong in this." Sanctification happens in our
soul, which we cannot touch or see with our physical eyes. It is only
when we look at the circumstances that God places us in that we get
clues about what he is sanctifying in our lives. But we cannot look
inward if we have a spiritual brick wall of pride blocking our vision.

One thing you must know is that whatever aggravates you in
someone else is the very thing that God has cleansed you from,
or is currently working on cleansing from your life. You may see a
trait in your neighbor that *gets under your skin.* If you pray and ask
God to reveal the reasons to you, he will give you a clear vision of
a time when you were guilty of the exact same sin that you so hate
in that person. And if this is not the reason, then it is that you are
weak in handling that particular situation and he is trying to make
you strong and stand up to that temptation with a perfected prac-
tice of his law instead of running away in defeat. Many times we be-
come hateful toward the people who offend us. We stop growing

because anger and hate take our eyes off of what God is trying to do in our own souls.

It is not easy to look inward to see if we are the problem because it takes a lot of humility. You take yourself down a couple of pegs when you ask the question, "Is it me?" And yet there are many who spend their entire lives blaming themselves for the actions of others. If this is where you are right now, stopping this action also takes humility; you have been convinced that all along you were on the right path, and it will take a lot to accept that you were in the wrong the whole time. No matter which category you find yourself in, know that you know nothing unless God gives you the information. All that we think we know must be crucified, and we are to ask the Most High to reteach us everything brand new as a child. There is nothing that we must think, say or do without first asking God to show us the right thing to do. We must be slow to react, and quick to ask him for liberty to act. Many people jump to think untruths and try to shame others instead of patiently waiting on God to direct them to act in love.

Everyone has a story. All it takes is a few minutes of talking with someone to learn about an experience that shaped who that person is today. There is a reason why people act and think the way they do, and most often it is rooted in childhood experiences. The thing is that many of us do not get to this level with people because we are either too impatient to take the time to listen, or we are too ashamed to share the truth about our own experiences (past or present). Many times we are quick to judge once we get a snippit of information about someone. People will usually give a little information about themselves to see what the response will be, before proceeding to give the real meat of their life story. Many do not pass this test and end up repeating to others what was told to them. And instead of really knowing the people we live and serve with, we find ourselves stuck at the "Hi and Bye" level with our neighbors. All of these reasons cause us to have a broken fellowship, and God's work of sanctification becomes stalled.

I urge you to ask him to show you the reasons for the people in your lives before you make conclusions that are far from the truth. We do not know what he has sanctified in or out of someone's life, or what weaknesses your neighbors are still struggling with. Therefore, conflict is bound to occur in our fellowship. If we ask God to teach us how to see and love like him, our own sanctification will reach new heights and we will be able to fellowship based on a higher level of wisdom. We must therefore learn how to engage our neighbors in conversations based on a genuine care for them, and be more ready to listen than to speak. Only God can give us this ability, so we must pray and ask him to guide everything that we think, say and do with the people in our lives. The Most High tells us in scripture over and over again to love unconditionally, to think kindly about others and ourselves, and to walk by faith and not trust our own understanding.

Friend, there is no way that you can tell just by looking at someone where they have been, where they presently are, or where our heavenly father wants to take them to. You just can't, so stop trying to "figure people out". Instead, work out your own issues, for they are many! In scripture, our personal issues are compared to a beam in our eyes (Matthew 7:5). Let us ask God each day to help us take this log out of our own eyes before we try to judge others. Am I saying that we should not talk to other people about their struggles, and just focus on ourselves? No, but in our daily walk our focus must be on how our heavenly father is guiding us personally and on what he expects us to learn in the situations we find ourselves in, instead of being focused on understanding other people's sins. In this approach we will learn to love like God loves, see as he sees, and to base all of our actions on his principles of truth. When we do this, we surrender to his process of sanctification. And as we surrender to his process of cleansing, our fellowship will be marked by less conflict. Our interactions with others will then become a nurturing and fulfilling experience in spite of conflict.

I hope that you have a greater knowledge of what fellowship and sanctification mean. Realize that on this journey of life we need the strength of each other. To have this strength we must build each other up, not tear each other down. Our enemy is in our midst encouraging us to fight so that we'll forget the true reason we are here: to claim victory over the sin in our own lives so that we can be a blessing to others, regardless of the differences in our culture or the color of our skin. May we surrender more and more each day, and may God's work of sanctification be made complete in each of us!

In what ways are you a better person today than you were before? List any improvements or changes that you can see in your life? (No matter how small, it is vital that you take time to be thankful for the work that God has done/is doing in your life).

Fourteen

TOTAL SURRENDER TO GOD

"But without faith it is impossible to please him: for he that cometh to God must believe that he is, and that he is a rewarder of them that diligently seek him"
— (HEBREWS 11:6).

Many times when we face the toughest challenges in life we ask: "Why me?" One day I was very overwhelmed with the stresses of work and as I prayed, I asked this very question: "Why do I have to go through these things?" In a calm way, the Holy Spirit replied: "Do you think I allow experiences into your life for no reason? The situations that come in your life are for you to grow and help others who have a similar need." That message was simple yet powerful and took my level of wisdom to new heights. I realized then that I had something worth sharing and I was encouraged to press on with writing this book. God opened my eyes, and in my mind I began to replay some of the most traumatic experiences of my past. They suddenly had new meaning because I finally saw his wonder-working power in all of them. Now as I look at my past experiences, I see that each of them teaches me a valuable lesson that I need as a woman, a mother, a wife and a teacher. There is no shame in growth!

We were created to walk step by step with God in this journey of life, for it is he who is the mastermind behind the lessons, the teachers and the tests that we encounter from day to day. Each soul undergoes specific training and is given unique tests. If we pass the tests we move on to a higher level than we were before; and this brings further training and tests. If we fail our tests, or don't complete our training, we must retake and redo them over and over again until we pass, not even with 99% mastery, but a 100. If God sees that there was even a hairline margin of error, our effort is counted as incomplete, and we must redo it again until our mastery is to perfection. We pass and fail in our minds because our minds control everything else about our souls. The world keeps us focused on the physical, but we must look **within** in order to have a personal encounter with the creator. When we inspect ourselves we see who we really are, and learn more and more about how we are being trained.

Ask yourself this question: why is everyone so unique? The obvious answer is that everyone is unique because each person was created for a unique purpose. Each person is perfectly created to do a work that no other individual can do. Everything that we have is so that we can each come to the Most High God in complete surrender. Instead of doing this, we look to what is taught through the media to tell us who we are and how we should be. We do this many times without considering that the companies that bring us this information did not create us. How can we expect people who didn't create us to know what's best for us and the purpose of our lives? Still many souls live each day, believing that the body they see in the mirror is the true them, and that mainstream media is right in telling them what they need in order to feel and look better.

We often beat ourselves up when we realize that we cannot ever live up to the standards of the world, and we end up using food, *drugs*, sex or suicide as a means of escape. Many more sink into depression and end up in an institution on the quest for happiness. The Word is very clear about how valuable each soul is. All of creation was designed for a purpose, and each person adds a special part to the whole. And I will say this again for emphasis: you were created and endowed with a unique combination of resources and abilities because there is a unique work that our creator has for you to do that no one else can do! Each one of us is a perfect fit into his master plan! That is why you were given life! There is no such thing as an accidental birth, so remember always that you are a special piece of the universe.

Not quite convinced? Then here's another question to consider: If we were not valuable, why would spiritual beings attack us to no end? You might say, "I am a Christian and I cannot be affected by any other spirit." If you have this thought I urge you to put this book down for a moment and read chapter twelve of the book of Matthew. If we are not affected by spirits of destruction why would Paul, the writer of several books in the Bible, say:

For though I would desire to glory, I shall not be a fool; for I will say the truth: but now I forbear, lest any man should think of me above that which he seeth me to be, or that he heareth of me. And lest I should be exalted above measure through the abundance of the revelations, there was given to me a thorn in the flesh, the messenger of Satan to buffet me, lest I should be exalted above measure. For this thing I besought the Lord thrice, that it might depart from me. And he said unto me, 'My grace is sufficient for thee: for my strength is made perfect in weakness.' Most gladly therefore will I rather glory in my infirmities, that the power of Christ may rest upon me. Therefore I take pleasure in infirmities, in reproaches, in necessities, in persecutions, in distresses for Christ's sake: for when I am weak, then am I strong (2 Corinthians 12:6-10).

When I first read this passage, I was confused. I had to stop, pray and ask God to help me understand the meaning of it. It took several weeks for me to get an answer. I am convinced that it took that long for an answer to come because I was filtering **truth** through the incorrect teachings I collected over the years. The Holy Spirit revealed to me that there are several kinds of beings which move about us without being seen. I was taken back to the scripture in chapter six of Ephesians: "For we wrestle not against flesh and blood, but against principalities, against powers, against the rulers of the darkness of this world, against spiritual wickedness in high places" (Ephesians 6:12). This passage helped me to realize that there are many spiritual powers that rule over this Earth who try to establish control over us, in addition to the one *evil* force that we know as Satan or *the devil*.

Even though this message was clear to me, I still did not understand why Paul referred to the 'thorn in his flesh' as a "messenger sent by God". Does this mean that God sends us spirits too that make life difficult for us? The answer to this aspect of my question came months later. I was taken back to the story in Eden. In the beginning of their creation, Adam and Eve did not know the difference between good and evil. As pointed out before, everything made was seen as very good (Genesis 1:31), and our creator wanted things to remain this way in Adam and Eve's perceptions as well. That is why they were told not to eat from the tree of the knowledge of good and evil. Good and evil now exist as part of God's divine order, but this first pair of humans did not know the difference. Because of their interactions with sin in the Garden, our creator must now use these very devices to act as a means of bringing us back to him.

All of our experiences come about for us to choose whether or not we will obey God out of a love for him. I hope that as you read this book you will see that the power of choice is one of God's expressions of love toward us. Our ability to choose freely without him *strong arming* us and turning all of us into robots is what true love requires. But even with this gift of choice, he does not let things just happen in chaos. Everything is in order. He prepared laws that hold everything in place and let all of his creation function in order, even though we have some amount of freewill. He knew what Adam and Eve's choices would be, so he set the scene for it to happen in an orderly way. He also created a way back to himself, shown by Jesus Christ, which is also one of order.

Each individual soul must make a choice to love God, because one who truly loves would never force the one who they love to love them back. If you are a lady, would you want a man to force you to love him? If you are a man, would you want to force a woman to marry you? Similarly, "for God so loved the world, that he gave his only begotten Son, that whosoever believeth in him should not perish but have everlasting life" (John 3:16). God showed his love toward us first, like any creator who truly loves his creation would. It is left up to each person to decide how he or she will react to that love. Will you reject it or will you reciprocate God's love by loving him back? If you love him, then let him influence your every step.

Our creator is all powerful and can go up, down and around the 'corridors of time' and change what details he wants to change, however he wants to change it. He made us and he can do whatever he wants to do. When I first realized this, I wondered if that meant that God is selfish. But how could God be selfish when we are told that he is love (1 John 4:8). Now I know that even if he was selfish, it would not matter, because we are his creation, not his judge. This theme of God's sovereignty is clearly expressed in Jeremiah's revelation:

The word which came to Jeremiah from the LORD, saying, Arise, and go down to the potter's house, and there I will cause thee to hear my words. Then I went down to the potter's house, and, behold, he wrought a work on the wheels. And the vessel that he made of clay was marred in the hand of the potter: so he made it again another vessel, as seemed good to the potter to make it (Jeremiah 18:1-4).

As it is revealed later in the passage that the potter here is being compared to our creator, it is confirmation to us that God works on us as he sees fit. Now look at the second part of the story which gives a clear example of how his sovereignty works, as Jeremiah is instructed to prophesy against Israel and Judah:

Then the word of the LORD came to me, saying, O house of Israel, cannot I do with you as this potter? saith the LORD. Behold, as the clay is in the potter's hand, so are ye in mine hand, O house of Israel. At what instant I shall speak concerning a nation, and concerning a kingdom, to pluck up, and to pull down, and to destroy it; If that nation, against whom I have pronounced, turn from their evil, I will repent of the evil that I thought to do unto them (Jeremiah 18:5-8).

We should never take God lightly when he tells us of his abilities. We must grasp this urgent truth that there is an appointed time set for each of our body's death and there is a real place called hell which awaits souls who will continue to be rebellious. As children of The Most High God, we must be thankful for the time that he gives us to live, rest in the promise of eternal life in heaven, and devote our time here to living abundantly for him.

As parents, my husband and I have learned that there is a balance involved in raising healthy, spiritually fit children. On one side of the balance lies our desire for building a lasting relationship based on love and trust between us and our children, where they know that they can depend on our unconditional love. But on the other side of the balance we strive to establish respect and a healthy fear of authority. As God's children, we are expected to have the same balance and regard for him. The price he paid for us (the sacrifice that his love required) was costly, and he does not want us to take it for granted. So today, take another look into your mirror. Look for who you are deep within, and choose to let God lead you in each step you take.

At this point, I will encourage you to read chapter fifty one of the book of Psalms. Meditate on God's unfailing love and on the wonderful plans that he has for you. Ask him to prepare your mind to worship him in the true knowledge of who he is.

Jesus lived in total obedience to God. What parts of your life are not lived in total obedience (full surrender) to God's law?

What do you do, use or eat as a way of coping with the struggles of life?

Read over Psalm 51. What does this passage of scripture tell you about yourself?

What does Psalm 51 tell you about God?

Make a list of the times of the day that you feel (physically, emotionally, mentally or spiritually) strong?

Make a list of the times of the day that you feel (physically, emotionally, mentally or spiritually) weak?

Use these times to decide on times when you will devote to praying/ spending time with God.

Fifteen

THREE INSTRUMENTS THAT HELPED TO SHAPE ME

"Honour thy father and thy mother, as the LORD thy God hath commanded thee; that thy days may be prolonged, and that it may go well with thee, in the land which the LORD thy God giveth thee"
— (DEUTERONOMY 5:16).

Dear Daddy,
I wish you were here in person so that I can look you in the eyes and say thank you for all that you did for me and all that you tried to teach me. Hopefully I will see you in heaven one day so I can personally tell you the words that I am about to say. Even though I doubted it when you were alive, you loved me and wanted the best for me. In your own way, you showed me love. I could not accept it because as an idealistic child, I thought your love could only be shown by you always being kind to me, and by you never making mistakes. But you were a real person with a natural ability to sin, and be overwhelmed, just like the rest of us. You gave from the little you had, and you loved me the way you were taught to love. I really appreciate the legacy that you have left with me.

For many years I was resentful because much of what you said and did was influenced by the tough road that you walked. Yet, you valued education and were the one who told me that nothing but the best was good enough. It was you who gave me the drive to excel in everything that I put my hands to do. You taught me that life is worth enjoying and giving up is never an option.

When life got hard financially and I had to make jewelry and other crafts to supplement our income, I was told that you did the same when I was a child. You did whatever it took to make sure that we ate and dressed the best, and had a roof over our heads. Your drive to meet our needs made me the mother that I am today. You never gave up, no matter how sick you got and I will never give up, no matter what happens.

You remarried because you said that all hope was lost for you and my mother and I resented you for that. I don't resent you anymore, as I now understand as an adult how it must have felt to know that there was no hope of reconciliation between you and your wife. I took it to mean then that you did not love me, but now I know that you reacted in a way which you felt was going to ease the pain. That has taught me that I should never be quick to react, but always seek God's will first and wait. I live my life with your last advice to me etched into my mind, "Sometimes you have to give up your rights for the sake of peace." Those words have taken me away from many fights and given me much peace in times of conflict.

Daddy, how could I forget that it was you who threw my first birthday party at the age of thirteen? How can I forget that you took the little that you had and made a big deal about it, inviting my friends and cousins over? I am touched every time I think about how humble the meal was. It was all we had in the house, but you had it in your heart to do something special for me. How could I ever think that I wasn't loved? I love you daddy. I carry your torch of endurance and drive to survive in the midst of the storms of life. Wherever you are now, I want you to know that in many ways I am just like you. May your soul rest in peace!

Dear Mommy,

I thank God that you are alive and I have the opportunity to express my love and appreciation of you in person. You have sacrificed everything for us. You have worked all of your life to take care of the children in your care, from your siblings when you were a child yourself, to your own five children.

As a child I never understood the stamina that it took to wake up at 5am every morning to get four children ready for school, to then walk miles to get transportation to take you to your little shop miles away in the city. I was always eager to go to school and never missed a day. You did not talk much, but I did. You never once told me to stop talking. You just bowed your head over your knitting, while you listened to me chatter on about my hopes and dreams. Now as a parent of three children who talk as much as I did, I remember the kindness that you showed me and I try to be as tolerant as you were. Thank you for never giving up on me, and for not abandoning us.

The thing is, you never thought that there was another option. You went on with life as if taking care of your children was your job and nothing else mattered. Even when you came to America you could have chosen to forget about us, but you looked back. I don't know what sacrifices were made while you were here and we were in Guyana, but I know that you made sure to send money each month (sometimes several times a month) to take care of our needs. I am sorry that you and daddy could not reconcile your differences, but God used that situation to give you a second chance at life. I pray that you take this opportunity of life and ask God to show you what it is that he has prepared you for these many years. Maybe you need to speak to young women who are going through the same situations that you did and give them hope that putting your trust in God never fails.

I thank you for teaching me how to love my children. As a child, I thought that you were too strict of a disciplinarian, but now I know better. Your discipline made me a well-mannered, loving, selfless, fair and hard-working woman. These traits I now pass down to my children. You taught me how to keep my children clean and how to present them in public because of how you took care of us as children. We were never sick, and our clothes (even though were few in number) were always kept clean. We each had one church outfit at a time, until we outgrew it. At that time we got one more. You ironed our clothes for us on Sundays and encouraged us to go to church while you stayed home most times to cook and clean up. Because you had to work Monday to Saturday, leaving home at five in the morning to return at nine at night, the only time left was Sundays to do your household duties. So when we returned home from church, we found you bent over a huge pile of clothes in the yard, washing them. You have done so much for us.

Even though there was a lot on your plate, you never forsook the things of God and you helped to start a church in our village by letting them use our home for their first meetings. You did not stop there but took time to prepare snacks for everyone to eat. I remember being about five years old during that experience. When I was thirteen, it was through that same church that I made the decision to follow the way of Jesus Christ and asked God to save my soul.

I was a young adult when you remarried. I thank you for choosing a loving, responsible and respectful husband who never showed me anything but the love of a father. I thank you for choosing wisely, as I never experienced the horrors that many endured from an unkind stepfather. His legacy of unconditional love will always be remembered.

In spite of everything we experienced, you showed me that as a mom you could be both a no-nonsense disciplinarian and my best friend; I am able to use this as the model for my role as a mother today. For these and the many more that I have not listed, I thank you, sweet mother of mine! I am so glad that you are in my life and that I can tell you how much I appreciate you. I see you in my actions every day and I will pass on your legacy of strength, determination, and unwavering love of God to your grandchildren. Better days are yet to come!

My Dear Auntie!

Your sweet personality, big heart and love for books made me the reader, teacher and writer that I am today.

Your unwavering humor, love for children, and sincere care for everyone you come into contact with are traits that I too share!

Your vigor and energy, unstoppable spirit, loyalty and ever-present concern will always inspire me as I try to be a loyal wife and friend.

Your quickness in making up songs, and your gift with stringing rhymes to catchy melodies to get your message across have shaped the "funny" yet disciplined mother that I have become.

You took me in when I needed you most. You opened your doors to a child who desperately needed you to be there.

You did your best and I want you to know that the experiences you gave me made a lasting impact.

I know you won't want me to write a whole lot in honor of you, so this small tribute is just to say: Thank you!

Write a letter to your parent(s), other guardians, or a loved one, alive or who has passed away. Express your appreciation for all that they have done for you. (Getting your deepest feelings out on paper will give you closure, clarity and peace).

$\mathcal{S}ixteen$

EMBRACE YOUR UNIQUENESS

"Therefore if any man be in Christ, he is a new creature: old things are passed away; behold, all things are become new"
— (2 CORINTHIANS 5:17).

When I was ten years old, I knew things that other children my age, or even many adults, did not know. I often wondered why I was that way, but mostly kept it to myself. In that same year, my family experienced the tragic murder of my then eldest brother, who was eighteen years old. My spiritual awakening grew even more from that traumatic event.

I spent most of my free time with my elderly relatives, and I became much more comfortable because they listened to what I had to say and answered many of the questions that I had. When I read the story about when Jesus was a child, I made an immediate connection. In a biblical account of Jesus' childhood in chapter two of the book of Luke, twelve year old Jesus left his family's caravan and went to the temple where he questioned and reasoned with the elders. The same way that they were amazed to see a child with so much understanding about God and his laws, the old people that I spent time with listened to me with eagerness and encouragement. They got my jokes, and I was able to learn a lot more about life from them. Today, I still feel more comfortable speaking with people much older than myself. While I was being trained as a teacher, I learned that it is very common for some children to gravitate to older people, and even though I did not understand it at the time, this was very true about me.

Being more mature during the years of early adolescence, and naturally drawn to the elderly, I appeared different from most children my age. As time passed, I developed my own style and marched to the beat of my own drum. I never allowed anyone to tell me what I should wear, how I should live or how I should think. I questioned everything, so much that there were many instances where I stood up to authority figures when I felt like their actions were unjust or unfair. You can say that that caused me to feel somewhat self-righteous, and it is only recently that I learned from the Word that submitting to authority is a necessary part of obeying God.

As I got older, I became a perfectionist, because of the high standards that my father required of me, who saw my potential and pushed me to strive for excellence. Now I see that both of my parents wanted me to do better than they did and that affected the high standards they had for me. I never saw myself as special, but I had an inner drive that was further pushed by wanting to help my family. Within the last ten years of my life, God has given me some hard core challenges, which gave me a reality check that I am a sinner just like everyone else, and in need of his mercy and grace. I learned that I am nothing without my submission and total reverence to Almighty God and that I CAN DO NOTHING TO HELP MY SOUL WITHOUT HIS POWER!

I was broken to the point where I had to give up all of the thoughts and imaginations that once seemed fulfilling to me. One day I was sitting in my living room and I just started crying. The curtain of my self-righteousness was ripped from my soul and I cried a bucketful. Our heavenly father broke me only to revive me again and began a great work of renewing my mind. All I had to do was believe that I was valuable to him and let him do the rest. That day I realized that I did not know who I was. Everything I did and thought about myself up until that moment was based on what others had said about me and what I learned from the media and college. Like the hopeless and abandoned newborn baby that God recovered and cleaned up in chapter sixteen of Ezekiel, I sat confused on my sofa. As my husband tried to figure out why I was crying so intensely, I was just as clueless. All I knew was that I realized my confused state and was humbled that the one who created the universe created me as an image of himself. I didn't know why, but he wanted to recover what was lost and make me into a new person. That day, God started a work in me that I knew I had no control over. Today, I am spiritually, emotionally and mentally strong and I am a product of his transforming power. If he can take an insecure, people pleasing, anxiety filled person and turn her into a humble, calm soul who is excited about life and committed to serving him, he can do greater things for you.

Today, it is important that you search yourself and take a closer look at the uniqueness of your experiences, because it is through these experiences that God has tried all this time to get your attention. Start by listing all of your traits that make you feel different from others. Realize that most of what you think describes who you are, are actually coping strategies that you have developed to survive and interpret life. Family members and people you closely interact with will see things in you that you may not see in yourself. Of course not all of what others say about you is the truth. So before you do this activity, ask God for guidance.

Answering the questions below will give you some insight into your uniqueness and give you a glimpse of your true personality traits.

What talents or opportunities have you rejected just because you wanted to please others, or 'fit in'?

What makes you YOU? (List the traits that make you unique.)

What traits does God want you to have? They may be the same or different from the ones listed above. List them as God reveals them to you and determine in your mind that you will be the person that he wants you to be.

Seventeen

WALKING IN THE FULL ARMOUR

Finally, my brethren, be strong in the Lord, and in the power of his might.
Put on the whole armour of God, that ye may be able to stand against the
wiles of the devil. For we wrestle not against flesh and blood, but against
principalities, against powers, against the rulers of the darkness of this
world, against spiritual wickedness in high places. Wherefore take unto you
the whole armour of God, that ye may be able to withstand
in the evil day, and having done all, to stand. Stand therefore, having your
loins girt about with truth, and having on the breastplate of
righteousness; And your feet shod with the preparation of the gospel
of peace; Above all, taking the shield of faith, wherewith ye shall be
able to quench all the fiery darts of the wicked. And take the helmet
of salvation, and the sword of the Spirit, which is the word of God:
Praying always with all prayer and supplication in the Spirit, and
watching thereunto with all perseverance and supplication for all saints

— (EPHESIANS 6:10-18).

*A*s we learned in the previous chapters, our true battles hap-
pen behind the scenes of our daily experiences. Knowing
this, our creator in his wisdom prepares us for these spiritual

110

encounters by arming us with tools that have the potential to protect us from every unseen attack. As we learn to trust in the Most High God for guidance in every step of life, we must remember to put on the protective gear that he has provided to guide, guard and protect our souls. Let us take a closer look at the armor that God has given us to keep us safe.

In verse ten of chapter six in the book of Ephesians, we are first urged as children of God to be strong in him and in his power. Whose power do we have to be strong in? It is God's power, not ours. Too many times we say we have given him the power to control our lives, when in fact we hold on to the reigns really tight, thinking that we know best, and that the one person who we can truly depend on is ourselves. When people do things to offend us, we lash out without turning that person over to the power of God. Our creator is not a little imaginary fairy friend who sits on our shoulder hoping that we listen to him. He is The Most High God! In order to successfully fight, we must give him the controls of every part of our lives. How do we do this? First we must begin each day by asking him to take control of our emotions, our will and our thoughts. We must acknowledge that we do not have a perfect knowledge of who he is and who we are but all that we need has been given in his Word. Next we need to accept that we cannot count on ourselves or on others to know all of his principles completely because we have all been deceived by sin. We must then tell God that we would like to be free from the bondage of sin in our minds. Each day must begin and continue this way, where we ask him to deliver us, cleanse us and take full control over all aspects of our lives. Living in total surrender to God means using the tools that he has given us to be successful. When we keep our eyes on his principles, we are in his will and are exactly who he created us to be.

In verse eleven we are told then to put on the whole armor of God, so that we may be able to stand against the wiles of the devil.

As we learned, there is a group of created beings who chose to be disobedient to God. They believe that they can be independent of him and fight us. They are real and do real damage in our lives. These beings, which most of us cannot see, are very successful because they convince us that they do not exist and that our problems come from our own minds. Many scientists, who claim that we evolved, do not believe that these spiritual beings exist. They are convinced that our minds *play tricks* on us. To them, believing in anything outside of what can be seen would be proof that there is also a supernatural force that is in control (God), so their way of dealing with that flaw in their theories is to just believe that there is no spiritual realm. Does this way of thinking make any sense to you?

We see the effects of spiritual forces at work in the world as we watch the news. What would make someone put their child in a trash can and burn her to death? What would cause someone to feel like there is no meaning to life, kill their family, then commit suicide? And what would drive someone to go into a public place and kill innocent people? Yes some people have genuine *mental breaks*, but I can say with all certainty that the root cause of many of these activities is influenced by beings in the spiritual realm. If there isn't a real spiritual force at war with us, why would God tell us that we need spiritual armor? We should take even greater notice to the fact that we are not told to put on part, but the WHOLE armor of God.

In verse twelve of our opening scripture we are warned, "We wrestle not against flesh and blood, but against principalities, against powers, against the rulers of the darkness of this world, against spiritual wickedness in high places". As we observe people's behavior, we believe that they are our enemies, when they are actually being influenced by spiritual forces that are determined to hurt us. What we fight are powerful energies of various levels of power who choose the path of wickedness and evil. This is the darkness that this verse talks about. Note also that they are called spiritual powers and wickedness in high places. This tells us that the forces we fight are organized and are very powerful. It would be foolish of us to not believe this and decide to go about life with the idea that all that exists is what can be seen. It would be equally foolish to think that if we don't think about them, they won't bother us, when we are told in God's Word that we wrestle with them.

This information can make us very fearful, so we must remember that the Most High is in control. It is not for the faint of heart, and God has not left us hopeless and vulnerable to these attacks. Do not take this command lightly then when we are told "take unto you the whole armor of God, that ye may be able to withstand in the evil day, and having done all, to stand" (6:13). It is restated here in this verse again for emphasis that we MUST take on the WHOLE armor. The armor that it talks about is God's Holy Spirit. Think of how much we are loved and cared for that our creator would give us the best of what he has to protect us from our enemies. Whatever situation we are going through we are always to remember how much we are loved. We are told here that it is through the armor of the Spirit that we would be able to stand and not ever fall, no matter how powerful our attackers are.

We are not expected to hide from these forces of wickedness or to give up in defeat, because there is no escape. We are expected to take a stand, having our loins girt about with truth, and wearing the breastplate of righteousness (6:14). We must not sit in the midst of spiritual warfare, thinking that everything is ok. Nor must we lie down in defeat, believing that we have no control. We must stand, believing that the battle has already been won. Standing means that we are alert and ready to use God's armor in the appropriate way for the situation at hand. Our most intimate yet vulnerable area (our loins) is used here to highlight our most vulnerable spiritual area (our emotions) and we are told to gird it up with TRUTH! This tells us that our most vulnerable area is where our truth is attacked by lies.

We must resist the attack in our emotions by securing ourselves in truth, instead of letting our emotions run wild. Similarly, a soldier's breastplate protects his upper body from frontal attack that could otherwise prove to be deadly since many vital organs are found in that region of the body. Spiritually, we are instructed to put on the breastplate of righteousness. Just as we depend on our heart, lungs, liver and all the other organs in our chest to live, we must be totally committed to righteousness as if our lives depend on it. With every breath and beat of our heart, we must live in righteousness.

It is comforting to know that the full armor of God even covers our feet. In verse fifteen we are told to let our feet be "shod with the preparation of the gospel of peace". Note that even though we are given all the tools necessary to protect and defend ourselves, we are expected to walk in peace. This is telling us that we must first pursue the path of peace in all situations and when this does not dispel spiritual attack, we must be prepared to defend ourselves. Even as we are prepared to fight, we must be even more prepared to live in peace.

To be prepared to live in peace, we must be strong in our faith. We are told, "Above all, taking the shield of faith, wherewith ye shall be able to quench all the fiery darts of the wicked" (6:16). There are some interesting facts about a shield that we must remember: a shield is not to be put on, but to be held; it is not restricted to one place like the others listed so far, but can be moved to many other areas of the body to enhance protection, and to collide with any incoming attack. We are told to take the shield of faith above all else because the way we handle the rest of God's armor will depend on our faith. And when our enemies find our week areas, it is our faith that must come to our defense, reminding us of our beliefs in the Most High God. Our faith must be impenetrable, just as a strong shield prevents penetration of incoming attack. It is important then that we first figure out what exactly we believe about our creator's power before we attempt to engage in spiritual warfare. Some might say that they are not interested in finding out more about this spiritual armor because they just want to live life carefree, and that there is no such thing as spiritual warfare. Just as soldiers return home from war to find civilians going about life in total ignorance of the war they just fought, in the same way we are all caught up in a war whether we want to believe it or not.

We are then told to "take the helmet of salvation and the sword of the Spirit, which is the word of God" (6:17). A soldier's helmet is used to cover and protect the head. When the Word talks about our head here, it refers to our mind (the seat of our will). In the order that God established, **he** should control our will, and our will, shaped by its submission to him, should then control every other aspect of our being. Verse seventeen lets us know that above all else, we must determine in our mind that the victory is guaranteed and we will be saved! Salvation is God's plan for his children to live life in abundance while on Earth, and to have everlasting life through Christ. In our daily battles in the *spirit*, we must remember that we are saved through our faith in the life, death and resurrection of Christ.

Finally, we are to take the sword of the Spirit. Notice that the sword is the only part of the armor that we must use to attack the enemy. It is the Word that has the power to vanquish the lies that make the enemy flee. The sword, which is the Word of God, is truth. Like the shield, a sword is not held in one place in battle, but is used to strike in every direction. As we wear the full armor, and as we do battle in our own minds, never lift your finger, never open your mouth, and never approach the enemy without the Word of God. When we find the enemy in our midst (again you will know them by their fruits) we must not believe another lie that they spin, that maybe it is a figment of our imagination. Hold up the sword with all confidence and declare the truth of the Word of the Most High God. The forces of evil and wickedness know the Word better than us and it is the one thing that they fear.

Knowing this you MUST have an intimate relationship with God's Word if you are to use this sword effectively. This can be achieved by reading, studying, and meditating on it, and by letting it saturate every aspect of your life. Again, the undefiled Word of God is the only thing that defeats the principalities, powers, and wickedness in high places. Know this then that if you attempt to use the Word (the sword of the spirit) with an impure heart of unforgiveness, dirty hands from sinning, and a weak faith from not fully believing God, you will be seriously harmed. So please beware! Live forgivingly, love unconditionally, think humbly, and believe wholeheartedly. And whatever way God tells you to serve, serve faithfully.

Having been instructed on the uses of every piece of God's armor, we are told to pray and keep watch. We must be busy following the way of Jesus Christ, "praying always with all prayer and supplication in the Spirit, and watching thereunto with all perseverance and supplication for all saints" (6:18). In all instances of life, and in every conscious moment, we must be aware of our surroundings, our thoughts, and the activities of those around us, not in anxiety, but prayerfully with God's guidance through the still, small voice of the Holy Spirit. We must not wait to be attacked. Clothed in the full armor of God, we must pray. When we do pray, we must not pray as if the one we are talking to is bound in this physical realm, but acknowledge the total dominion and all-encompassing presence of God. Dwelling, moving, speaking and praying with the whole armor on is to live in Spirit and in truth. This makes us unstoppable, invincible and spiritually victorious no matter what we face. As a child of God, we were created with these traits. But in order to be these things we MUST put on the whole armor of God.

Read over Ephesians 6:10-18. Ask our heavenly father to show you which part of his armor you are not using correctly. Pray that he teaches you what must be done so that you can be fully protected and armed for spiritual warfare.

Make a list of what God reveals to you and continue praying and building this list. From time to time, check off answered prayers.

Eighteen

WHAT'S YOUR THEME SONG?

"Therefore if any man be in Christ, he is a new creature: old
things are passed away; behold, all things are become new"
— (2 CORINTHIANS 5:17).

Every soldier has a song,
Will you say that I am wrong?
Directions, data, motivations and coordinates to treasures,
Are all captured by the deliberate rhythms and rhymes of a song.
If this is not true, why are there marching bands?
Why the bagpipes, and why the cadence?
We were all created to have a song,
One that motivates our movements, prompts our
molecules to work,
One that points us in which direction to take when
we are at a fork.
Songs remind us of our history,
Reinforce the contents of our thoughts.
There are songs that mark the way back home,
Whether it's a hum, a whistle, or a groan.
Not convinced, look at nature.

Listen to the pitter patter sound of the raindrops,
The faithful crowing of the rooster,
The howl of the wind, the whispers of the forest,
The beats of your heart.
The buzzing of bees, the calling and answering of birds,
I could go on and on, and still couldn't describe all
of the many sounds of his creatures, both great and small.
Growing up, my big brother and my mother would sing,
My auntie could make up a song about anything.
My other two siblings sang their melodies from deep within.
I heard their cries, I heard their laughter,
and I watched as their hopes and dreams come alive later.
I recently discovered that even as I was singing prayers and praises all along,
It was my family's and friends' songs that maintained my drive.
"How can I help people?" was the theme song of my little heart as a child.
How can I right the wrongs, and wipe away my momma's tears when she cried?
Today when I am down to my last drop of strength,
I remember mom's solemn songs and sing to my heart's content.
If you don't deliberately come up with your song
That tells about who God is to you,
Or by his standards what you must do,
You will be given a song to sing, and they will not be for the best interest of the soul in you.
These songs will worship this world, and will contradict the Word,
They will glorify creatures, and not lift up the one creator.
You will curse yourself with these catchy spells,
or you will believe them in ignorance, or with foolish innocence even casually dispel.
You'll keep on singing the catchy notes, as the distance in your soul swells.

Sing a new song of praise to the Most High God,
And reteach your heart to sing for his glory.
Your soul will move to a different vibration,
To match a simple story,
Of hope, of truth, of salvation, of righteousness, and liberty,
Of joy and peace in the Holy Ghost,
Of God's sweet grace and mercy.
No matter what is going on in your life, never let your new Heart Song of Glory cease.
Use the words of God that you know, and write them upon your heart with peace.
Make up your own melody, and play it over to overwhelm the ones from your past.
Declare with your mouth, believe in your heart, "Through Jesus, I'm free at last!"
You may have different songs for different reasons,
But never let your praise be out of season.
Start listening to the things you say to yourself.
Is it: "I am no good", "I need something outside of me to look and feel good",
"I can't do anything right", "There is no hope for me"?
These are not just thoughts, but melodies you sing to create your life story.
My song that I sing now, when I am reminded of the wicked words I sang to myself in the past,
Is "Therefore if any man *be* in Christ, *he is* a new creature: Old things are passed away;
Behold, all things are become new".
"Yes I sinned,
But now I am saved and sanctified to serve,
Too busy to wander.
Not a slave to the sins of my past,
For God made me a fighter and a winner!"

What destructive thoughts do you say to yourself?

Ask God to heal you and give you a new "Heart Song" that is aligned with his Word. Today, start by writing down one or more Bible scripture that you've learned so far. Memorize it and say it to yourself when a self-destructive thought comes to mind.

Nineteen

Angels Among Us

"For by him were all things created, that are in heaven, and that are in earth, visible and invisible, whether they be thrones, or dominions, or principalities, or powers: all things were created by him, and for him"
— (Colossians 1:16).

In learning more about who you are as a child of God, it is very important to be aware of his spiritual workers who watch over us while we walk this road of life. In English we call these messengers: angels. Scripture refers to them mostly as *messengers of God.* Just like most other words, people of different cultures and generations have different names for these spiritual workers. So let us not get carried away with the word *angel* or with what we have been taught about them: that they are all winged creatures dressed in white, with a halo on their heads. We are taught by the mainstream media that angels look a certain way, but this imagery leads to a lot of confusion and continues to keep us further away from knowing the truth. Angels are often disguised to look just like a normal person. And they live, dwell and do things that will make us not realize who they are. Many times we interact with angels and do not even know it. This chapter is a very brief look at what scripture tells us about God's messengers.

The first fact I would like to point out is that scripture makes a clear differentiation between spiritual workers of righteousness who are obedient to God and spiritual workers of sin who are disobedient to him, generally called 'demons'. Let us first revisit the passage that reminds us of the unseen beings who we fight against, before we learn about the ones who work to help us. Paul writes:

"Finally, my brethren, be strong in the Lord, and in the power of his might. Put on the whole armour of God, that ye may be able to stand against the wiles of the devil. For we wrestle not against flesh and blood, but against principalities, against powers, against the rulers of the darkness of this world, against spiritual wickedness in high places" (Ephesians 6:10-12).

The Holy Spirit shows us through this passage that when we think that it is people who wrong us, we are actually all influenced by forces which we cannot see. We are ALL in some way tempted by destructive spirits who are in disobedience to God but parade around us as if they are our companion and have our best interest at heart. Remember once again that no matter who is disobedient to our creator, he has ultimate control of everything because as our creator, all is subject to his will (Colossians 1:16). His spiritual law, which can be summarized into the seven principles of truth we looked at in the beginning of this book, serves to judge all of his creation, create perfect order, and maintain his complete dominion over all things. We must therefore set out to do exactly what God tells us to do at all times.

Now that we have established the fact that there are disobedient spirits among us who mean us great harm, be consoled that God has a spiritual army of workers who watch over us, making sure that those who choose to obey him remain in his perfect will. Knowing this, we must never get caught up in fighting the forces of sin by our own devices. Instead we MUST remember to be clothed in the full armor of the Most High God, which is simplified by living the way of Jesus Christ and walking in the Spirit. And we must bravely take a stand for purity and righteousness knowing that we are never left alone, but surrounded by an army dedicated to keeping us safe. The rest of this chapter is dedicated to these, our co-laborers of righteousness.

First we must know that angels communicate with God and have a perfect understanding of what he wants for us. In the book of Hebrews a simple question is asked, after the writer talks about the might of God and his relation to angels. He asks, "Are they not all ministering spirits, sent forth to minister for them who shall be heirs of salvation?" (Hebrews 1:14). We see from this that angels know who will inherit salvation, and know what each of God's children need. They are sent to guide and bring us back to his law. We are told again in the book of Psalms, "The angel of the LORD encampeth round about them that fear him, and delivereth them" (Psalm 34:7). When you are in crisis, and attacked by the workers of unrighteousness, just remember that we have an army of workers of righteousness striving to deliver us from harm. In order to benefit from this protection we must remain obedient to God. Whatever you do, I urge you to purge your minds of the information and images that the world has given about angels, and other subjects and let the Holy Spirit give you truth according to the Word of God. If not, you will take what God tells you and filter it through the lies that you have been taught, and what scripture says about his messengers, or about anything else, will not add up. If you do not ask him to cleanse you from these lies and teach you the truth, you will reject his messengers that are sent to help you.

There are various types of angels with different responsibilities. Each person has their own set of angels that work behind the scenes carrying out God's divine plans for each soul. They work both in the physical and spiritual realms, while life happens around us as we go about our day to day tasks. An example of how angels function is seen in the book of Acts where Peter wakes up in his prison cell and finds that his chains have broken off of him, while his cell was locked and heavily guarded by a Roman soldier (Acts 12:5-10). There are many other instances in scripture where angels brought messages to people or watched over them in times of trouble (Genesis 19, Genesis 21, Genesis 22, Exodus 14, Matthew 4:11). While we have the Holy Spirit of God working on us from within, we have angels busy at work around us.

Angels who obey God are fully committed to following his law. I will give you two passages from scripture to prove that angels are in communication with him at all times, and that even though sometimes he changes what he asks them to do, they still remain obedient. One example is found in the first book of Chronicles, where God tells his angel to communicate with then king David that he has a choice of three punishments to pay for his disobedience (1 Chronicles 21:6-16). The angel communicated this to David and he chose the punishment of having Jerusalem taken over with a plague for three days (21:13). While the angel continued the killing of the soldiers during the plague, God saw David and his people's repentance, and ordered the angel to stop killing them (21:15). The next example I will give about the angels' ongoing and open communication with our creator is found in the book of Zechariah. In chapter one of this book we read about an angel who asks God how long he will continue to be patient with the disobedient people which the angel was observing (Zechariah 1:12). When we think of angels, we generally don't consider that they are in constant communication with God, but they are.

One other very important detail we must remember about angels is that they can change forms. We are told in the Bible that these messengers might appear to be people destitute and in great need. Similarly, we are told in scripture that Satan and his followers masquerade around us as angels of light (2 Corinthians 11:12-15). We are taught then to not practice favoritism, choosing who to accept and reject based on outward appearances. "Let brotherly love continue. Be not forgetful to entertain strangers: for thereby some have entertained angels unawares" (Hebrews 13:1-2). How can we tell the difference between a messenger of God and a follower of Satan? We are given the answer in the book of Matthew:

Beware of false prophets, which come to you in sheep's clothing, but inwardly they are ravening wolves. Ye shall know them by their fruits. Do men gather grapes of thorns, or figs of thistles? Even so every good tree bringeth forth good fruit; but a corrupt tree bringeth forth evil fruit. A good tree cannot bring forth evil fruit, neither can a corrupt tree bring forth good fruit. Every tree that bringeth not forth good fruit is hewn down, and cast into the fire. Wherefore by their fruits ye shall know them (Matthew 7:15-20).

And how do we know what fruit to look for? Once again the Word provides the answer. The "false prophets" might be portrayed as the righteous members of our community, while the true messengers of God may come to us as simple persons of poor means. The attributes that we must look for are love, joy, peace, longsuffering, gentleness, goodness, faith, meekness and temperance (Galations 5:22-23). This list is a simple breakdown of all of the attributes of the law and can be used as your test to tell if someone is of righteousness or not. Notice that what they offer you or encourage you to do (their fruit), must possess ALL of the above traits for it to be of God. If you are being told something that will bring you joy, but breaking God's law will be the result, refuse it and walk away, no matter how enticing that thing is. If you keep being tempted with it, face it, and hold up the sword of the Spirit, declaring the true Word of God, as in the above passage from Galations.

Today, I hope that God opens your eyes and show you that he is real and that his workers are real. May we all be humbled by the magnitude and glory of his creation around us, and learn to rest knowing that his workers are among us working out his divine order. May we learn to look at the things and the people in our surroundings with new eyes, as we ask God to show us what it is he needs us to think, say or do in each moment. Do you see now how valuable you are to our creator? Ask him to forgive your pride in thinking that you have dominion over your life. Ask him to give you new eyes to see the boundless beauty, and appreciate the awesomeness, of his creation. Ask him to help you to be aware of the angels in your midst. And remember to always thank him for everything. If you are a parent, then you know how it feels to have children with a thankful attitude. That is what our humility and thankfulness mean to our heavenly father. Know this then that God and his messengers see our hearts, and inspect our growth. Whether you will believe it or not, we are being carefully analyzed to see if we are fit for eternity with Christ. The days of believing worthless things about ourselves are over! As children of the Most High we must wake up and know that he is real, he is good, and his mercies endure forever! A right knowledge of who we are in relation to God should bring us to perfect humility, perfect obedience, and perfect faith in him.

What experiences have you had in life that could not be logically explained, or you knew just could not be a co-incidence?

Part Three

Why Was I Created?

And God said, Let us make man in our image, after our likeness: and let them have dominion over the fish of the sea, and over the fowl of the air, and over the cattle, and over all the earth, and over every creeping thing that creepeth upon the earth. So God created man in his own image, in the image of God created he him; male and female created he them. And God blessed them, and God said unto them, Be fruitful, and multiply, and replenish the earth, and subdue it: and have dominion over the fish of the sea, and over the fowl of the air, and over every living thing that moveth upon the earth. And God said, Behold, I have given you every herb bearing seed, which is upon the face of all the earth, and every tree, in the which is the fruit of a tree yielding seed; to you it shall be for meat. And to every beast of the earth, and to every fowl of the air, and to everything that creepeth upon the earth, wherein there is life, I have given every green herb for meat: and it was so. And God saw everything that he had made, and, behold, it was very good. And the evening and the morning were the sixth day (Genesis 1:26-31).

Twenty

THE POWER OF PRAYER

"Ye lust, and have not: ye kill, and desire to have, and cannot obtain: ye fight and war, yet ye have not, because ye ask not. Ye ask, and receive not, because ye ask amiss, that ye may consume it upon your lusts"
— (JAMES 4:2-3).

"Be careful for nothing; but in every thing by prayer and supplication with thanksgiving let your requests be made known unto God"
— (PHILIPPIANS 4:6)

"Confess your faults one to another, and pray one for another, that ye may be healed. The effectual fervent prayer of a righteous man availeth much"
— (JAMES 5:16).

"And this is the confidence that we have in him, that, if we ask any thing according to his will, he heareth us"
— (1 JOHN 5:14).

We are hopeless if we do not pray. We are defeated if we do not pray. We rapidly decay if we do not pray. We will be controlled by the spiritual powers of wickedness if we do not pray. We are worthless if we do not pray. Our life becomes a field of death and destruction if we do not pray. We will lose our greatest asset- our soul- if we do not pray.

Why is prayer so important? Prayer is important because it is the language of creation. All of life's various forms of energy is manifested and maintained by the deliberate use of words, which is prayer. Prayer is the universal language of all creation because all of creation was made by the Word of God. So whether we want to believe it or not, we all pray. When we obey God, we pray according to his will and our prayers are answered, for he will not make anything happen that will contradict his goals; this would be chaos. When we do not live according to the will of our creator, our prayers go unanswered.

We live with the belief that we have many choices, when in fact we only have two in each and every experience: obedience or disobedience to God. While we are busy during the course of the day with our *gismos* and *gadgets,* we unknowingly utter all forms of prayers, and these words manifest things into our lives and reveal our most intimate thoughts. Know then that in the course of our day, we either pray to God in obedience, or in disobedience to him, we pray to the forces of wickedness. We send out prayers into the universe, continuously affecting what is brought into our lives and the lives of others. We must recognize the power that we weild and deliberately set our minds to obey the will of the Most High God. It is when we come face to face with this wonderful ability to communicate with our creator, and realize that he answers our prayers when we are in his will, that we will pray with wisdom, purpose and power.

How do we pray with wisdom? We must first stop and ask God to show us what is the purpose for each and every experience in our lives. Part one of this book prepares us for effective prayer by laying a foundation of who God is and how his principles work. We must now use this foundation of knowledge to understand what he wants from each of us. When we pray, our thoughts must always match truth or we will be praying in vain or destructively; God cannot contradict himself. Be very careful then how you open your mouth and utter words, because as is written in the introductory passages above, he hears everything and determines our level of growth based on what we say, whether outwardly or in our minds. He then rewards us accordingly.

How do we pray with purpose? God shows us that we are his Word manifested into physical form. To pray with purpose, we who are created in his image must be deliberate when we pray. We do this by first establishing a special time and place for prayer. The place chosen must be easily accessible, clean and solely dedicated to spending time alone with God. Some people call this place a prayer closet, but the size and location does not matter. Once this area is chosen, spend some time in it, either alone or with other loved ones, praying and asking God to fill it with his presence. Ask him to always reveal his perfect will to you, and tell him that when you are there you will always be honest and remember his power and sovereignty. Ask him to always remind you to put on his whole armor (the power of his Spirit) and teach you how to use every aspect of it wisely. Finally, ask him to bind the enemy and give you discernment to recognize when you are being attacked, so that you will have the courage and power to overcome.

The list below gives more information on how to pray with purpose.

1. Establish a time or several times of the day that you will stop and pray to God.
2. Before you pray, clean up if you are messy.
3. Keep your prayer area clean and clutter free.
4. Your cleansing must be both spiritual and physical, so do not begin praying until you forgive those who have offended you and ask God to forgive you of your sins.
5. Be thankful. Tell God thanks for the resources and experiences that you have.
6. Ask him to show you what he expects from you in the matter that you are praying about, then state your desires in detail and according to his principles of truth.

7. End all prayer with thanksgiving and humility, knowing that what God wants he will get.
8. Expect an answer. It might be "yes", it might be "no", or it might be "wait".

You may copy these strategies and place them in your designated prayer area, or anywhere else that you choose.

How do we pray with power? In order for our prayers to be answered, faith is essential. We must study what God says and believe that his Word is true. We are to recognize that as his children we have great power and be totally surrendered to his will. Also, as noted in number six above, praying with details is very important. If you are praying for a spouse, and you ask for a hardworking man, or a beautiful woman, don't be angry if God gives you that and only that. When I was looking for a church, I made a list of twenty things I was looking for, including that it should have a Jail Ministry. To many my requirements seemed overwhelming and pompous, but that church was delivered to me with the exact details that I prayed for. Just like I made an impossible list of expectations for a church, I made a similar one for a husband. God gave them both to me just as I asked. When we pray for our needs we must honestly tell what we are willing to compromise with, and what factors we would struggle to accept. Our heavenly father will not be angry with us for being honest. And doing this will prepare us to face the challenges that we might experience with our answered prayers. If it is God's will, our request will be given just as we asked.

We must forgive others before we ask for anything because of God's divine law of forgiveness. If we do not forgive we will not be forgiven, and our prayers will not be answered. When we hold grudges, we judge his perfect law and call it imperfect, and this is sin (James 4:11-12); God's Word tells us that he does not work with sin. We cannot expect to have a powerful prayer life, or to be in the will of God, if we are judging his law. But through forgiveness our prayers will be aligned with his plans. As noted before, our creator does not answer prayers that are against his will because that would be chaos. For this reason, forgiveness is necessary in having a powerful prayer life.

I will stress again that in order to have a powerful prayer life, we must believe! It is vital that we believe in God's presence, his promises and his power. Our emotions, when used correctly, fuel our belief, which in turn fuel our prayers. The more we believe God, the more enthusiasm and hope will be released in our prayers. The more we feel in need, the more zeal we will pray with. And the more desperate we feel, the more we will be inclined to drop on our knees and cry out with intensity. Let us ask God then to show us how to use our emotions effectively when we pray.

If you do all of the above you will have wisdom, purpose and power when you pray. But even with this success as a prayer warrior, you will still be attacked spiritually. You will either be attacked directly in your mind, or indirectly through the people in your life, because the enemy will be furious that you are trying to tear down their strongholds. They will use family members, friends, co-workers, even church members to attack you. Don't give in to these attacks. Pray! Think of all of God's promises and do all the things that his Word tells you to do. Put on the whole armor of God, exercise your faith, expertly use the sword, and the enemy will flee.

Watch out for any thought, whether it comes from someone you know or an unknown source, that goes against God's principles of truth. Even though these thoughts or inspirations are camouflaged as comforting or for our best interest, if they go against the Word in the slightest way, run. Run fast, and run far from them. As you put on the full armor of God, prepare to take a stand. If you need an example of one who took a stand, walking always in Spirit and in truth, focus on Jesus. He knew the Word intimately, took a stand for righteousness, never sinned, and had a faith so strong that he defeated death. His blood is a force to be reckoned with and it bought our salvation. So whenever you are told that your life is not worth anything, that your hope of eternal life with Christ is not guaranteed, or that you are free to sin, remember the blood that was shed for you and pray.

The book of Psalms, which is mostly accredited to King David, is a great model for our prayer life. I urge you to read the psalms, especially in times of great danger and tribulation. Some very powerful prayers are found in chapters 3, 23, 27, 51, 91, 93, 94, 119 and 139. Many consider the book of Psalms to be just songs, and people have even created songs based upon many of them. As we learn in chapter eighteen, our innermost prayers become the songs our hearts sing. So it is very hard sometimes to tell the difference between a song and a prayer. When I was a little girl, the older people said time and again that there was power in the psalms. When I read the book of Psalms as an adult, I realized that the words could only have been uttered by someone who had a deep connection to God, and who knew their place in relation to his power. The writers were true prayer warriors. You can tell that their hearts were pure, their hands clean, and their minds were clear when they uttered those words to the Most High God. They knew that they had to forgive totally and leave all judgement to his mercy and grace. Even though many of the chapters reflect the presence of grave danger, the faith of the psalmists was astounding. They truly believed that God had the power to deliver them **IF** he wanted to. They knew that at the end of the day he alone determines if, and how, he will give us the desires of our hearts. The fact that God gave us 150 psalms should be enough to tell us that they are important. The prayers/ songs in the book of Psalms, including the ones listed above, are perfect examples of how we should pray. I urge you then to study and meditate upon them.

Our prayer life is not a public thing but an individual relationship between each one of us and the creator. No one can force someone else to pray for it is a personal choice to use this gift that is individually given to all. We either choose to pray to God and be a survivor on this battlefield, or we can ignore him and be a casualty of spiritual warfare. We are expected to be more and more skillful in prayer, but we each must make the choice.

Before we go any further, know that even though we are talking here about setting a special place and time for prayer, prayer is the soul's preoccupation. We are always praying! A soldier has designated and specific assignments, but once a soldier, always a soldier. In the same way, we should not only wait for designated times to pray, but be aware of our thoughts and emotions throughout each day. Praying deliberately with wisdom, purpose and power is not just for yourself, but will help you to effectively intercede for the other people who occupy your life. And when your *neighbors* are strong, they will be able to help you and pray for you when you are weak.

A final point that must be stressed about prayer is that it is a two-way conversation. God is not far away, but lives in you through his Spirit. So even as you talk to him, acknowledge that he is really there and take the time to listen to him as well.

What area of your home can you set aside for prayer and spending time with God?

What time(s) during the day can you set aside for prayer and spending time with God?

Choose one thing that you would like God to give you. Ask him to give it to you if it is his will. Be very specific by listing as many details about this thing as possible. Remember to return to this page periodically and check off if it was answered.

Twenty One

THE POWER OF FASTING

Wherefore have we fasted, say they, and thou seest not? wherefore have we afflicted our soul, and thou takest no knowledge? Behold, in the day of your fast ye find pleasure, and exact all your labours. Behold, ye fast for strife and debate, and to smite with the fist of wickedness: ye shall not fast as ye do this day, to make your voice to be heard on high. Is it such a fast that I have chosen? a day for a man to afflict his soul? is it to bow down his head as a bulrush, and to spread sackcloth and ashes under him? wilt thou call this a fast, and an acceptable day to the LORD? Is not this the fast that I have chosen? to loose the bands of wickedness, to undo the heavy burdens, and to let the oppressed go free, and that ye break every yoke? Is it not to deal thy bread to the hungry, and that thou bring the poor that are cast out to thy house? when thou seest the naked, that thou cover him; and that thou hide not thyself from thine own flesh?

(ISAIAH 58:3-7).

—

Fasting enhances the fuel of our prayers!
It sets the captive free.
It asks God, "Why not me?"
It says to our almighty creator, "So shall your will be!"

139

"Use me, help me, strengthen me, so that I might serve you
faithfully."
Giving up is not an option,
When to our every temptation, we press on, falling
a victim to none.
Our eyes are lifted up,
When not bowing down to a bowl or a cup.
Our hearts are stirred up in pain,
Slowing down to our own individual lusts,
Speeding to catch up to God's Holy Spirit again,
Letting every principality and power know that our confidence is
in a new master;
Giving God full control makes everything clearer.
Repairing, renewing, reshaping, relieving,
Restoring the temple to its readiness to receive God's presence-
his full power.
Oh the wonder to behold!
The power restored!
Ready to conquer,
Able to intercede for others.
Surrendered to the Most High God:
Greatest, wisest, master, teacher and healer.
This is what fasting does for every believer!

What day can you set aside for fasting?

What will you give up while you fast?

Who will you pray for while you fast?

Is there anyone in need that you can help while you fast?

Twenty Two

One Path Leads to God!

"Enter ye in at the straight gate: for wide is the gate, and broad is the way, that leadeth to destruction, and many there be which go in thereat: Because strait is the gate, and narrow is the way, which leadeth unto life, and few there be that find it. Beware of false prophets, which come to you in sheep's clothing, but inwardly they are ravening wolves"
— (MATTHEW 7:13-15).

Today there is global scale deception, and very subtly, many souls are being led away from a life committed to God. Without being aware, many are lulled asleep by technology, science, and a movement which teaches that a conscious effort to commit one's life to God is not necessary. It is urgent then that we keep our eyes focused on our salvation through Jesus Christ and on the hope of eternal life with God. The more we get caught up with the cares and the affairs of this world, the less we think of what happens to our souls when our bodies die. The fears, the technology and the teachings of this world are very convincing and cause us to be stagnant in our spiritual growth. Know three things: 1. the one who created us created technology! He put it in our minds to conceive such things and all technology is built from natural resources in nature, which God created. 2: science is man trying to make sense of our world. It struggles to accept the belief in a supreme being because no one can put our creator in a lab and study him. Learning about God is based on faith, and many scientists will only believe what they can prove based on the observations of their five senses. 3: the religious movement which teaches that all paths lead to God is not correct with this belief, even though **some** of its other teachings are actually based on divine principles of truth. After considering these points, we are left with the simple choice of obedience to a wise, all- powerful creator, or disobedience to him.

Man continues to ask the question: "Why are we here?" Are we alive to just exist, meditate and live life however we want to? Are we here to party and enjoy life until the day of our death? Is this why the miracle of our conception happened when our daddy's sperm fertilized our mother's egg? And for those who believe in evolution: why did some soil got together and formed a fish, to form a frog, to form a monkey to form a half human to form us today? How is it that soil, water and sand still remain and did not all evolve? The intricate magnificence of birth could not be a mere coincidence. Everything about nature shows a resourceful and wise creator, and not the product of chance. Everything, no matter how tiny, serves a purpose.

Our bodies were perfectly designed for our souls to fulfill God's purpose. If you find this hard to understand, we are told, "Before I formed thee in the belly I knew thee; and before thou camest forth out of the womb I sanctified thee, *and* I ordained thee a prophet unto the nations" (Jeremiah 1:5). Clearly, we are told that we were known before we showed up on the scene of Earth. I have been told by many scholars that this means that

God planned how he was going to make us before time began. Whatever the case is, this passage tells us that he knew us and planned the purpose of our lives before we came to Earth

Because we all inherited sin and experienced death because of Adam and Eve, it is only by our choice to accept life individually, that we each will have eternal life in heaven. That is what life is about- the opportunity as an individual soul to make the choice of surrendering entirely to the will of our creator, thereby inheriting the gift of eternal life. The movement today that teaches that all paths lead to God, and that hell is just a metaphor to describe the experience of pain that we experience here on Earth, promises that we could have a utopian society if everyone seeks out the goodwill of men. They believe that it doesn't matter what church you go to or who you worship; we all will be in union with God one day. Some of their teachings are biblical. Others are close to the truth, but are lies. Many are falling for this teaching because they do not take the time to study the Word for themselves. We are told in God's Word time and time again that there is only one truth and one narrow path to everlasting life, but wide is the road to destruction (Matthew 7:13-15). God created everything, so indeed, we are all somehow connected to his Spirit. However, the Bible teaches that there is only one path that leads to eternal life with him; this is by salvation through following the way of Jesus Christ.

At the core of this movement is the belief that the only evil is what we imagine in our minds. Once again its message is very close to the truth; we are told in the Bible that God did not want us to have the knowledge of good and evil. While writing this book I was constantly attacked by thoughts of doubt. And these attacks proved to me that evil does exist, but indeed, God never expected us to know it. Neither did he want us to know "good" as defined as the opposite of bad or evil. He expected us to know only obedience! Whatever he commanded us to do, he expected us to be like the trees, the animals, the oceans and the air, and just do it.

While writing this book, I stumbled because of those doubts. But my faith in God was strengthened the more I saw how he worked through me. His Spirit gave me the hope to press on and complete this work regardless of my challenges. And as I dwelled in his full armor, I became better at spotting the enemy's schemes for what they were. Writing this book taught me how to GROW UP and take a stand for righteousness with unshakeable faith.

The difficulties that I've experienced as I try to live righteously tell me that there is no way that there can be total elimination of conflict on Earth by just the actions of men. Everyone naturally want to believe in a world of perfect peace, happiness and love, and this would be possible if we were not up against spiritual forces who really exist and create havoc in our lives. I cannot tell you how many different realms there are, but because of my personal experiences with spiritual attack, I can say that I agree with scripture which differentiates between two realities- the physical and the spiritual (Matthew 4:4, Ephesians 6:12). In these passages of scripture, we are clearly told that we have physical and spiritual needs, and that there are physical and spiritual beings who exist among us. We can form groups with people who all share our beliefs and values of life, but we will still not escape the forces of wickedness among us. We learn from the news often about groups who move away to form communes and did not escape the influence of sin. Even God removes his hedge of protection from around us sometimes so that we may experience crises in order to learn needed lessons.

While we are here on Earth, no matter where we run, we will always engage in spiritual battles. Jesus is the answer that God provided for us. He sent Jesus to show us the relationship we can have with him. Jesus also came to show us all that we can be, by completing the work that God sent him here to do. As we study his relationship with our heavenly father in scripture, we learn about the power we have when we have faith in God. Jesus showed us what we are up against as he himself endured temptation by Satan (Matthew 4:1-11). We see a perfect example of what it means to sacrifice our will in order to do our heavenly father's will, and how we must endure great pain sometimes as the cost of our obedience to him. But Jesus showed something else that should encourage us beyond measure. He showed, through his resurrection, the glorious manifestation of the true and enduring promise of the love of God, that when we die with our souls dedicated to obeying him, there is a glorious life awaiting us after death! In his ministry, Jesus simplified the message of how to obey God. Let's consider the answer he gave when a disciple asked him to tell which is the greatest commandment in the law. Jesus answered, "Thou shalt love the Lord thy God with all thy heart, and with all thy soul, and with all thy mind. This is the first and great commandment. And the second is like unto it, Thou shalt love thy neighbour as thyself. On these two commandments hang all the law and the prophets" (Matthew 22:36-40). Note the forms of the nouns used in this passage: law is singular, prophets is plural, and commandments is plural. What does this show? Jesus confirms to us here that there is only **one** law. Even though there are many commandments, many principles and many attributes of the Spirit, there is one law, one Spirit, and only one truth! Only one way leads to complete harmony with God, and that is through following the way of Jesus Christ, whose life, death and resurrection showed us the fulfillment of God's law.

Many people might use the sentence above to prove that all is one and therefore all paths lead to God. Scripture says something that is close, but fundamentally different. The Word tells us that there is only one path which leads to everlasting life (John 14:6), the path to everlasting life is narrow and few find it (Matthew 7:14), and that the Most High will oversee the outcome of every soul during the time of judgment (Revelations 20:11-15). This and many other passages show clearly that God has full control over all of his creation and has a time set aside for our final judgment.

What do you believe will happen to your soul when your body dies?

Twenty Three

Are Some Sins Worse Than Others?

"For all have sinned, and come short of the glory of God."
— (Romans 3:23)

efore we go any further, it is necessary that we clarify what *sin* is, because just like everything else, the world has a different version than the Word about what it is. This misunderstanding causes the believer and the non-believer alike to drift further from God in our minds. *Sin,* according to the Bible, starts in the heart and happens when someone determines that he or she can function outside of the law. To show that sin begins in the emotional center of the soul (the heart), let us look at what we are told in scripture:

Let no man say when he is tempted, I am tempted of God: for God cannot be tempted with evil, neither tempteth he any man: But every man is tempted, when he is drawn away of his own lust, and enticed. Then when lust hath conceived, it bringeth forth sin: and sin, when it is finished, bringeth forth death (James 1:13-15).

From this passage we see that sin starts with us being tempted to make a choice based on our emotions. Our main goal in life should be that we give God full control of our mind. When he controls our mind, our emotions suddenly are put into check and the mind has a better control of them, instead of them having control over the mind. Instead of reacting based on our emotions, we will then consider God's will, knowing that he only wants the best for us. We are further reassured of his goodwill toward us in the promise that "Every good gift and every perfect gift is from above, and cometh down from the Father of lights, with whom is no variableness, neither shadow of turning" (James 1:17).

We are then given instructions on how to keep sin at bay. "Wherefore lay apart all filthiness and superfluity of naughtiness, and receive with meekness the engrafted word, which is able to save your souls" (1:21). Each person is responsible for making the choice to accept these words and be a watchman for his own soul. We cannot just hear and know what God's Word says; we must also commit our lives to practicing it. Even though we all are capable of sinning based on our desires, we must have faith in God's divine principles of truth and submit our emotions, our will and our thoughts to his commands.

Our hearts should mourn and our will humbled when we consider the greatness of our creator's love toward us in spite of our sins. Some of us sin because we don't know better nor realize the far reaching effects of our actions. And some of us sin in spite of knowing better. All of us sin, just by the thoughts and feelings we entertain, or by simply refusing to act in spite of having a true knowledge of God (1:22-25). We see here that sin is any thought that is against truth.

Some might say that it is drastic to think that we can sin in our thoughts. Know that all thoughts, when given the ability, have the potential to be manifested into action. Sin creates a separation between us and God in our minds because in ignorance we don't see that everything is created to work in perfect harmony. Instead, we think that we are able to do things outside of him, ignoring the truth that his Spirit is in all of his creation. I find it interesting that *sin* in the Spanish language means "without or separate". In a nutshell, sin is simply a thought that something can exist outside of God's law. We are clearly warned that if we break one law, we are guilty of breaking the entire law (James 2:10).

When I think of God's love, my soul cries out to him in humility and worship. When I think of his compassion toward me in spite of my sin, I see the need to forgive people of their sins. I cannot hold hate or hostility in my heart when everyone else is experiencing the same challenges with sin as I do. Everyone has a different struggle with sin, but there is no sin that is worse or better than another, "for all have sinned, and come short of the glory of God" (Romans 3:23). How can I judge someone, when if it wasn't for God's choice to open my eyes to his truth I would have been in the same situation as that person? And how many sins do I commit unknowingly, causing me to need the forgiveness of others?

When we believe that we can choose our own life's path, our ignorance turn to arrogance and we are filled with pride (a lie, which is sin). Then we project this pride outward and curse others who are not *up to par* with our standards and accomplishments, as if someone made us the standard by which to judge others. As already mentioned, we play a part in the choices we make, but it is God who answers the desires of the tongue of man (Proverbs 16:1 and 9). There is an unseen force around us guiding our movements, encounters, and experiences. The Most High has already seen what is in our hearts and has therefore planned all of our paths. But we choose whether we will keep that old heart, or be transformed by letting him renew our mind.

God has already seen our destiny because he created our souls. He knows by the end of life as we know it on Earth who will choose to unite with him, and who will choose to remain in sin. As a result, he has orchestrated everything to work for the good for those who love him and choose to obey him, "And we know that all things work together for good to them that love God, to them who are the called according to his purpose" (Romans 8:28). Note that in this verse, the first prerequisite for things working out well for a person is the love of God. Whatever is in our hearts will determine what experiences our creator allows into our lives. And so we must willingly submit to him so that our hearts can be acceptable in his sight. The next prerequisite is that the person is called according to his purpose. Since God sees our hearts even before we were born, he calls us according to **his** purpose.

It is a dangerous thing to think that we exist outside of the control of our creator. Many people eat, drink, drug and depress themselves to their graves because of the sins of their past, thinking that there is nothing that can redeem them from the wrongs that they have done. This is not truth. See these thoughts as the lies that they are. Maybe you did something in your past and you think that it is absolutely unforgivable. There is a three-fold problem with this approach to thinking: First it is prideful to think that your or anyone else's actions could take someone out of God's control. Secondly, this destroys our internal strength. This erred way of thinking disconnects us from experiencing the full power that comes with a will that is in tuned with his will. Thirdly, this creates an open door for the enemy to come in and create strongholds in our minds, which will take great effort to undo once that stronghold is established. Could this be why the Word tells us over and over again to think virtuous thoughts and fill our minds with truth? At the end of the day, we each have to make the choice of what we will believe.

Today, ask God to strengthen your will. Repent of the belief that your sin, or the sins of others, are bigger than his power to save and redeem. He says that when we confess our sins, he is faithful and just and will forgive us of all our sins, and cleanse us from all unrighteousness (1 John 1:9); if we say we have no sin we deceive ourselves and the truth is not in us (1:8); for all have sinned and come short of the glory of God (Romans 3:23). All of us, every single day, in some way or another, believe that we are righteous in some area and not prone to a particular sin. This comes into play when we judge someone or judge ourselves when we, or they, do not add up to our own thoughts of what righteousness is. This is sin.

Let us dig deeper into the sin of pride. Before reading this, you may have thought that pride was just self-righteousness or rightfully seeking praise for doing good work. You may have also thought that the worse sins are pedophilia, fornication, and murder. The Most High shows us that pride is sin just as any other sin. Pride is sin because it is a thought that takes your mind out of God's truth and in your imagination separate you from experiencing the fullness of his Spirit. We were not created to be separate, but to function as part of the whole of the entire creation. So little by little, the thought of separation in our minds turn to extreme loneliness. And we were not created to be lonely so this feeling of loneliness could lead a person to take his own life or take the life of others. This happens because the temptations that that person entertained affected his emotions, which then weakened his connection to the Holy Spirit. The spiritual forces which we fight then hold the reigns over that soul's mind and cause the person to do whatever they want him to do.

God is everywhere, and there is nowhere that we can go and nothing that we can do to escape his presence and power. Proverbs 15:3, Matthew 10:29-30 and Romans 8:38 will give you more information on this truth. Satan thought, and still thinks today, that he could operate outside of our creator's master plan. But God created Satan and has a plan for him as well as every other one of his creations (Colossians 1:16, Romans 11:36). I searched the Bible over and over again for the reasons of Satan's expulsion out of heaven, and all of the references I found point to the fact that he became prideful and ambitious and wanted God's authority and position (Ezekiel 28:16-19, Isaiah 14:12-17). So let us be very careful not to undervalue the sin of pride which can destroy us just as fast as any other sin can.

One of the greatest tools of deception that our enemy has is their ability to convince us that some sins are worse than others and can't be forgiven. Any time you have questions about the sins of your life, talk to God about them and he will reveal the answers to you. If you are beating yourself up with self-pity, know now that this is a form of pride. Pick yourself up out of your bed of depression and get ready for the purpose your heavenly father created and prepared you for! Study the Word. You can start by studying each of the passages of scripture presented in this book. It is essential that you get your own Bible and take time to study the words of God for yourself. I strongly urge you to use the King James Version because it is the most accurate English version to date. Know that you are a soldier in God's army of righteousness, created to conquer sin, but you cannot conquer anything until you learn to carefully and expertly handle his Word.

Notice that while our enemy tells us that some sins are worse than others, digging deeper in the Word tells us something different. We are told that there is one sin that is unforgiveable and that is the blasphemy against the Holy Spirit (Matthew 12:31-32, Luke 12:10, Mark 3:29). It has not yet been revealed to me how we can do this, but what I can say is that if the forces of evil, who know the Word of God better than we do, know that there is a sin that is unforgiveable, they will focus their energies in getting us to commit that sin. Let us then humbly and completely devote our lives to the Master so that we will not blaspheme his Holy Spirit.

Over and over again we are warned in the Bible to focus on thoughts that are pure, beautiful and righteous, because our heavenly father knows that when we think of negative thoughts and thoughts of lack, it causes us to take off his protective armor. We are then left exposed to all forms of spiritual attack. We are created with the same creative force of God since we are made like him, and so our thoughts are seeds which when sown produce either life or death. When we entertain negative thoughts about ourselves or others, we create open wounds for sin to enter and systematically eat away at our souls. We must remember then to put on, and keep on, the whole armor of God.

Living burdened by the terrors of life is not an option for us. As unchained children of the Most High God we are marked with the blood of the lamb that was slain for us. We can confidently rest in the hope of life after death with Christ. This is our helmet of salvation. We must be armed with the Word at all times, which we have intimately studied, so that we can expertly and skillfully use it when we are tempted to sin. In unshakable faith, we must believe that there is nothing that comes into our lives without God first allowing it, and that there is no sin that he cannot pardon, unless it is blasphemy against the Holy Spirit. He saw our potential to sin from the beginning, and he came in the form of Jesus Christ as the perfect sacrifice to pay for ALL of his children's sins. He did this so that if anyone of us chooses to turn to him, we would be saved.

Repent today! Ask God to take full control of your life. Study and focus on his principles of truth. Slow down, accept his salvation through Jesus Christ and be the *you* that he created you to be, one moment at a time.

What sins have you done that you believe are unforgiveable?

Make a list of the aspects of your life (physical or spiritual) that you need God to heal?

Twenty Four

PAINFUL EXPERIENCES CAN

BRING US CLOSER TO GOD

"My brethren, count it all joy when ye fall into diverse temptations; Knowing this, that the trying of your faith worketh patience. But let patience have her perfect work, that ye may be perfect and entire, wanting nothing"
— (JAMES 1:2-4).

Growing up, there were periods of sadness as there were times of happiness, and all of those experiences made me the person that I am today! We can all agree that there were moments in our childhood, and our past, that we wish we could forget. But the enemy keeps our minds fixed on the sad memories and on our failures, drowning out the happy ones. While we wallow in our own pity party of could-have-beens, time zooms by. Why do you think this is the case? I find that a vital part of abiding in the full armor of God is the daunting task of focusing on the happy memories and thinking positively about the sad ones. As a little girl, I worried about my parents, who struggled in their marriage. I even worried about my family's financial troubles. No one knew it then but I was internalizing all of the family's problems, and spent a lot of time thinking about how our lives could be different. Instead of enjoying the simplistic innocence of childhood, I spent a lot of time thinking about the needs of others. As I got older, I became very resentful. This ungrateful attitude continued until I realized that it was all for my good, and that the care that I have for people is a part of the work that I came to Earth to do. I must now learn how to channel my concerns for myself and others in the way God intended.

It was in the process of writing this chapter that I realized that as an adult I also spent much time worrying about the welfare of others and thinking about how I could make people's lives better. God had to teach me the tough lesson of letting it all go and letting him bare my burdens. He showed me that in every circumstance of life, my job is to seek his will and to focus on what he is teaching me. When we do not give our problems over to God and ask him to reveal his will to us, our lives become a burden. When we do not seek his Word for the answers to our problems, we live in bondage to these experiences. I am here to tell you now that ignorance of the Word is the main way we remain in bondage to sin. Not studying scripture will leave us vulnerable to the strongholds that attempt to bind our souls. We must shift our focus to the loving, gentle, healing words of our heavenly father and learn to see everything though his loving eyes.

When I accepted the plan of salvation through Jesus Christ, I not only accepted the gift of eternal life, but God began to establish control in my mind. When I learned that he sent Jesus to show me the way, I fell in love with my creator on a whole other level. It was then that I started my lifelong quest to find out more about this wonderful being who created me. I started to read the Bible with an intense passion at the age of thirteen, and the more I read the more I was comforted. There was a period where I stopped reading God's Word and going among other believers, and I paid dearly for this. In 2010, I was reawakened, and realized how far I had drifted from his protection. I recommitted my life to following the way of Jesus Christ. I asked God to take full control of my life, and since then my spiritual growth has taken flight.

In 2010, I went through a period where I was very angry at myself for the length of time that I lived as a prodigal and in ignorance of what I meant to God. As I read his Word, I started to see that I was not the only person that went through periods of drifting from his presence. Living for him has been a bumpy journey, but it has been a consistent one that continues to strengthen my faith. Now when I face a challenge, even an inward prayer causes God's workers to show up and make my dreams come true in a way that I could have never predicted.

I feel loved and treasured as I live for God. He has given me a wonderful life partner and four precious children. In living with them, I see the benefits of the painful experiences of my past and know now that everything I go through is for my good. I take time out to reflect on the happy memories, and let God show me the truth and balance that the sad ones represent. My anxieties that came from being a people-pleasing-perfectionist are gone! I live as he carries my burdens. My mind is at peace and my soul is at rest. I am free, and my shackles are gone! I accept the new life which God bought for me with the blood of Jesus Christ, and his grace truly is sufficient for me.

When you ignore God's words, or don't follow them exactly as they have been given, you reject to use parts of his armor. You will know then that your armor has been compromised because you will feel fearful, hopeless and defeated. When you feel this way, know that you are seriously in harm's way. God never meant for his children to be defeated. At this point you must realize your need to be restored. Troubleshoot to find out which part of your armor has been compromised by carefully assessing the thoughts that fill your mind. Knowing scripture is essential for living this life because it is through the Word, and through the law, that we are able to arm ourselves. Never take matters into your own hands, but always ask the Most High to reveal his will in all things. From the tiniest detail to the big decisions of life, seek his will. Sometimes when we go through tough times, the enemy will show up and offer us an option that is attractive to our emotions. Knowing the Word of God intimately gives us the right reaction to these temptations and keeps us from succumbing to sin.

The struggles we experience from day to day have the potential to mature us and bring us closer to God. But many times we don't see a full victory because we are in a hurry to be set free from them. We take these experiences for granted or curse them as "bad" because society tells us that we deserve all the happiness that money can bring. The spiritual forces in our midst tempt us to focus on the negative aspects of our life situations. Instead, we must be thankful to God, having faith that he allowed those experiences into our lives to make us grow. We must then humbly ask him to reveal what the reason is and let him show us how to react. When he shows us, we must obey immediately instead of thinking that we have time to get it right.

Make a list of some painful or uncomfortable experiences that you've had in your past?

Make a list of some painful experiences that you currently have?

Thank God for these experiences as opportunities to learn and grow. Then ask him to show you their purpose and what he needs for you to do next?

Twenty Five

THE PARABLE OF THE WEDDING BANQUET

MATTHEW 22:1-14

Summary: Many of God's children lose their inheritance in his kingdom because their gifts and talents (the things he has given them) become stumbling blocks to their relationship with him.

While Jesus lived on Earth, his life's work was to declare the Kingdom of God and point us to the way back home to our creator. He used many short stories to teach us the principles of the Kingdom. We call these stories parables. In this and the next seven chapters, we will study eight of Jesus' parables to uncover some vital lessons that he wanted to teach us.

In the first parable we will look at, the kingdom of heaven is compared to a king who planned a wedding banquet for his son. The king had previously invited the people of status and wealth of his kingdom to the celebration. He "sent forth his servants to call them that were bidden to the wedding: and they would not come. Again, he sent forth other servants, saying, Tell them which are bidden, Behold, I have prepared my dinner: my oxen and my fatlings are killed, and all things are ready: come unto the marriage" (Matthew 22:3-4). You would think that after all of this, these highly valued and supposedly loyal associates of the king would show up. Instead, "they made light of it, and went their ways, one to his farm, another to his merchandise: and the remnant took his servants, and entreated them spitefully, and slew them" (22:5-6). When the king heard about what happened, he was angry, "and he sent forth his armies, and destroyed those murderers, and burned up their city" (22:7). Imagine all of this happening while the preparation was already made and while the king waits anxiously for his guests to arrive. Now imagine how angry and embarrassed the king must have felt. These initial invited guests were not just simply punished, but they, and their belongings, were completely destroyed.

The king then said to his servants, "The wedding is ready, but they which were bidden were not worthy. Go ye therefore into the highways, and as many as ye shall find, bid to the marriage" (22:8-9). People who were not the king's first choice were now his last resort. "So those servants went out into the highways, and gathered together all as many as they found, both bad and good: and the wedding was furnished with guests" (22:10). This had to be a very short time for these poor people to acquire clothes fit for a king's presence. Nevertheless, we are told that when the king came down to look at the guests he was shocked to find that there was one man who wasn't dressed properly. I am led to believe that the king provided a means for his poor citizens to be dressed for the occasion. Otherwise, his response simply would not add up based upon our human understanding. The king said to the unkempt guest, "Friend, how camest thou in hither not having a wedding garment? And he was speechless." (22:12). At this point the king is absolutely furious and orders his servants to bind the guest hand and foot and cast him into outer darkness where there will be weeping and gnashing of teeth (22:13). The story ends with the powerful lesson that many are called but few are chosen. Many may become uncomfortable in considering the king's actions. But just what does this parable mean?

First of all, remember two important points. First, this is a story that represents the reality of our current state, which is still in progress. Second, God already knows what will happen in the end because he reveals it to us through this parable. He is therefore using this parable to show his children what will happen to those who blatantly reject his invitation and his process of sanctification, and to give a promise to those who will accept his invitation and follow his instructions. There are many who continue to ignore God's call and claim that they are too busy to respond to his invitation. They have the knowledge, the resources and everything needed to develop a closer walk with him, but their preoccupations with their possessions become stumbling blocks.

Many people of 'faith' fall into this category because their outward religious practices are stronger than their inner connection to the Word of God. Outwardly they lead lives that would make you think that they are more inclined to righteousness than most. Some of them even sit next to you in your place of worship. God sees their rejection of him in their hearts and further extends his invitation to those considered rejects: the poor and the scorned from all corners of the Earth who may not have much to offer. These people, when they come to God, are the most humble and appreciative of his mercy and grace. They eagerly follow his will with a greater passion than those who were exposed to the Word of God all their lives. Notice with the unkempt guest that God does not expect us to remain as we were when we first hear his call. He expects us to know that we are in the presence of royalty and that we are called to conduct ourselves as part of a royal priesthood.

This story clearly teaches the lesson that no matter what walk of life God calls us from we are to present ourselves to him with dignity and respect. We must conduct ourselves everyday knowing that we are in the presence of a majestic sovereign creator, always giving him our best! This lesson is seen with the one guest who came in with inappropriate clothing for the feast. I am imagining that this man walked in with the smelly, raggedy clothes that he would walk the streets with. This is where maturity in faith is important in pleasing God; we must truly believe him in order to worship and obey him. And in order to be faithful, we must first know the details of what he wants from us. We have to know what kind of "king" he is so that we can truly please him. Considering the harsh penalty that the king punished this guest with, I got to thinking- what if this man was unable to get money to buy the appropriate clothing for a wedding feast? Maybe if he had known that his clothes would have offended the king, he wouldn't have gone to the feast dressed like that. However, my defense for this man cannot stand.

First of all, he must have heard what happened to the noblemen of the kingdom, and how the king showed his wrath and had them all killed. Secondly, the king asked him in verse twelve, how it was that he got into the feast dressed that way? This tells us that the king's servants guarded the entrance of the feast, and the unkempt guest had to enter by some not-so-ordinary means.

I tried to understand this with my own limited understanding, forgetting for a moment that this parable speaks of a time in the future with an ending that is yet to come. We are warned that God and his workers are taking note of how we are responding to his call. Even though we have all of the information needed, some of us will still not listen, and believe that the issues of our personal lives are more important than an invitation from God. We have been given the resources necessary to teach us to choose correctly, and each of us will pay for the choices that we will make.

What is in your life that makes it hard for you to make time to pray?

What is in your life that makes it hard for you to make time to go to church?

What is in your life that makes it difficult to make time to read God's Word?

What changes can you make today to have more time to pray, go to church or read God's Word?

Twenty Six

THE PARABLE OF THE WORKERS IN THE VINEYARD

MATTHEW 20:1-16

Summary: God has prepared a way for all of his children to receive the same inheritance of eternal life, regardless of when we accept his invitation for salvation, provided we do the work that he has called us to do.

In this parable, the kingdom of heaven is compared to a landowner who went out early in the morning to hire laborers for his vineyard (Matthew 20:1). The landowner had an agreement with the laborers who he first hired that their payment was to be a penny a day. The story continues that about three hours later he went out and saw others standing idle in the marketplace and told them, "Go ye also into the vineyard, and whatsoever is right I will give you. And they went their way" (20:3-4). Three hours later the vineyard owner went out again and hired more men who he found standing idle in the marketplace and gave them work. Once again, the landowner went back to the marketplace and saw more laborers standing around. He asked them why they were there standing idly by. The laborers answered, "Because no man hath hired us". He once again told these people to go and work in his vineyard, and

167

that whatsoever is right is what they will receive (20:6-7). We see up to this point that these laborers were hired at various times of the day, and that they each had an agreement with the landowner.

This story, like all parables, is filled with mystery, and only those with eyes to see and ears to discern can understand the meaning. Why didn't the landowner hire all of the laborers at the same time? Also, why did the man keep going to the marketplace over and over again? He had at least one other servant than the day laborers, yet he patiently went looking for people who needed work. Some of them must have been lost among the crowd in the marketplace and he therefore did not see them to hire them. Or maybe they came late to the marketplace. Some of the details are left out, but be assured that this is a story that gives us clues about the life we are actually living right now. Just as the servants were seen and called at different times, the same way we are born, and we are called, at different times. And even though we may be living in different places, or called to work in different locations, there is one that calls us, the Most High God, and one work that we are called to do, work in his kingdom and have a covenant relationship with him. We all are promised the same reward: God's approval and the gift of everlasting life! Just as the servants in the story were paid the same wage, the same way God's children, who choose to answer his call, will reap the rewards no matter when we are called.

Now let us look at the ending of the parable to see how the servants reacted to their pay. As you can imagine, there were some complaints about how much they were paid. The laborers who were hired earlier complained that they should not get the same amount of pay as the workers who were hired later in the day. The landowner replied:

"Friend, I do thee no wrong: didst not thou agree with me for a penny? Take that thine is, and go thy way: I will give unto this last, even as unto thee. Is it not lawful for me to do what I will with mine own? Is thine eye evil, because I am good? So the last shall be first, and the first last: for many be called, but few chosen" (Matthew 20:13-16).

God's kingdom is compared with this story of laborers so that we can know that he sees all of his children who answer his call as equals, even though the amount of work we do and the times of our calling may be different.

At first glance we may look at the behavior of the workers and accuse them of having a bad attitude. But a closer look at them will show us our own reflection; we also murmur against God concerning how others are rewarded. Do we truly know that he loves us equally? What did we sign up for when we chose to serve him? Which one of us says, "I will surrender to your will God, but on my terms"? Surrendering to his will means total agreement to **his** terms. Many people become angry when they have worked harder than others on their team, and everyone on the team gets the same grade or reward. We must avoid this confusion and focus on our own personal relationship with the Most High God. Does the Earth complain about the sun being higher in the sky? Do elephants and whales complain about why one's habitat is the sea and one the Earth? Do the clouds argue with each other because they sometimes merge and share the same space? Some might say, "I love God, and I know he loves me, but why does he love her too, when her work is not as good as mine?" When we do this we accuse the person of stealing something from us, and accuse our creator of not being fair, when everything is his to do as he pleases. I will tell you a simple truth: everyone's blessing looks different because everyone's burden is different, but God's love for each one of us is equal. Our eye becomes *evil*, as written in verse fifteen, and we no longer see truth, but evil, when God never intended for us to know evil in the first place.

To avoid falling into this pit of jealousy and resentment, let us ask God right now to use this story to open our eyes to see if we are like the murmuring servants. May we develop a relationship with him that is intimate, and which does not depend on the way he treats his many other children. We must settle in our hearts today that everything is his, and he can do whatever he wants with whomever he wants, whenever he wants (Job 41:11, Psalm 24:1). Don't let him have to take away all that you love for you to understand that all that you have belongs to him. We must watch out for fear and ask God to replace our fears with faith. You may wonder what fear has to do with jealousy. Fear is the root of jealousy because fear is what tells us that we are not loved or appreciated as we should be, and that someone else sharing our love will cause us some type of harm. Ask the Most High God to fill you with faith!

What are you afraid of?

Ask God to show you how you can replace these fears with faith. Write down what insight he gives you.

Twenty Seven

THE PARABLE OF THE WHEAT AND THE TARES

MATTHEW 13:24-26

Summary: God has allowed everything to work out the way it has in his kingdom, and continues to let sin have its course until his people have matured to perfection based on his judgement. Then the sinful and the righteous will be separated.

*I*n this parable, the kingdom of heaven is compared to a sower who sowed good seeds in his field. But while his workers slept, his enemy came and sowed tares among the good seed (Matthew 13:24). When I first read this parable I thought that tares were just regular weeds that we find in the yard that sprout up in places where we would rather other plants to be. But the more I studied this passage, the more I realized that there had to be a deeper significance of tares. One day, to my surprise, my Pastor preached on this parable and explained what tares really are. From his sermon I learned why the landowner instructed his servants to wait until the wheat reached maturity to dig up the tares from among them. Tares look exactly like wheat until they are mature. While the wheat bares fruit, the tares bare nothing, and this is the only way you can tell them apart.

The next point that must be noted is that the enemy came and sowed the tares while the men slept. If these men were awake and saw the enemy sowing tares, they would have tried to stop him. Knowing that the landowner here is compared to God, we may wonder why he allowed the enemy to come in at night as opposed to during the day time. The quick answer to this is that he has a purpose for everything, and allows everything to happen in divine order.

Naturally, the servants were upset when they finally saw the tares growing, and said to their master, "Sir, didst not thou sow good seed in thy field? From whence then hath it tares?" (13:27). He explained that an enemy had done this, and instructed the servants not to try to pull out the tares, but to leave them until the right time, or the wheat will be accidentally pulled up as well (13:28-29). Notice that the householder, as he is called in scripture, already knew what happened. Not only did he know what happened, but he allowed it to happen. This lets us know that God knows all that Satan is doing, and he has planned everything out just as he wants it. This parable also comforts me that our creator has a divine purpose for everything that happens in our lives. He wants us to grow to full maturity and will do everything that is necessary to safeguard and protect us.

Let's now consider what the householder tells his servants next. He says, "Let both grow together until the harvest: and in the time of harvest I will say to the reapers, Gather ye together first the tares, and bind them in bundles to burn them: but gather the wheat into my barn" (13:30). For quite a while I asked the question: Why does the owner of the field want his servants to dig up the tares first? The answer is that the wheat could not be removed with the tares left to be burnt up in the field because according to the custom during the time of Jesus, the fields were not fully harvested; a portion was always left back for the poor in the community. Jesus gave a more thorough explanation of this parable to his disciples when the larger portion of his audience left. When they asked for the meaning of the parable,

He answered and said unto them, He that soweth the good seed is the Son of man; The field is the world; the good seed are the children of the kingdom; but the tares are the children of the wicked one; The enemy that sowed them is the devil; the harvest is the end of the world; and the reapers are the angels. As therefore the tares are gathered and burned in the fire; so shall it be in the end of this world. The Son of man shall send forth his angels, and they shall gather out of his kingdom all things that offend, and them which do iniquity; And shall cast them into a furnace of fire: there shall be wailing and gnashing of teeth. Then shall the righteous shine forth as the sun in the kingdom of their father. Who hath ears to hear, let him hear (Matthew 13:37-43).

The explanation of the wheat and the tares cannot get any clearer than this! We are told here that there are people in our midst who are not who or what they seem to be. They grow alongside us, but not everyone is a child of God. There are people in our midst that are Satan's and they do their father's work just as well as their father. They are an excellent counterfeit but they are nothing more than that. This is not the first time that Jesus said that Satan is the father of some. Consider the dialogue between the Pharisees and Jesus in chapter eight of the book of John for your own reading. For the sake of this chapter, we will look at verses forty three and forty four where Jesus replied to the people who questioned him:

Why do ye not understand my speech? Even because ye cannot hear my word. Ye are of your father the devil, and the lusts of your father ye will do. He was a murderer from the beginning, and abode not in the truth, because there is no truth in him. When he speaketh a lie, he speaketh of his own: for he is a liar, and the father of it (John 8:43-44).

We need to be watchful and attentive. We are told that God's children hear his voice and follow him, and that many will say on the day of judgement that they have done great works in God's name. But they will be told that he does not know them.

Even though we read these words, we go about life not even noticing the powerful meaning behind what we read. Why would God say that he will not know some people? This is because he knows that there are people who are not his. Are some not his because they have set in their minds that no matter what they are taught they will not obey? Or are there demons that were influenced by Satan so that they reached the point of no return with God? This is one of those things that we know in part and must wait until we are face to face with God to fully know. But rest assured that scripture makes it clear that there are counterfeits living among us, but their days of causing death and damnation in our lives are numbered.

Are there challenges in your life that you want God to remove now? Write a letter to him, telling him about what is making you uncomfortable, and ask him to reveal how you must react to your discomfort?

Twenty Eight

The Parable of the Hidden Treasure

in a Field Matthew 13:44

Summary: From the very beginning, God saw that his creation of man was a great treasure. Even though he knew we would fall, he believed that we were something worth holding on to. So with the high price of the sacrifice of Jesus Christ, he paid for our safety and hid us in a way which we cannot understand, for the perfect time of our revelation.

In this parable the kingdom of heaven is being compared to a man who found a great treasure in a field. He hid it back again and sold everything that he had to buy the entire field. I believe that the man who found the treasure is God, and that the treasure is man. He knows our true worth, but the real value of who we are remains somewhat hidden from those who he felt he needed to hide us from. Several forces in the universe have been put in place to keep us protected and safe. There is a lot that we do not understand, because it is hidden from us until all of God's appointed plans for his creation are fulfilled. Since he is in control of all things, he not only has a purpose for us, but has a purpose for Satan and his followers as well.

When it says that the man sold all that he had, I believe this refers to the birth, death and resurrection of Jesus Christ. We are an investment and God sent Jesus as a sacrifice for us. We are special to our heavenly father and he has gone above and beyond our wildest dreams to preserve our safety. Scripture tells us: "What? Know ye not that your body is the temple of the Holy Ghost which is in you, which ye have of God, and ye are not your own? For ye are bought with a price: therefore glorify God in your body, and in your spirit, which are God's" (1 Corinthians 6:19-20). This passage confirms that the treasure that was hid is us, temples of the Most High God. Being sovereign, he looked through time and saw his children of all generations and knew each of us by name. He saw our fallen state but we were still important to him. So he bought back our immortality, and has us somewhat hidden until the day comes for our full redemption.

I thank God for choosing me! It is a humbling thought that he would think of us as worthy of the sacrifice that it took to buy us back from the hands of death. He bought us from the condemnation of his own law. Some of us might feel that we are, or even Satan is, in control; but our creator holds everything up with his law of truth. When we go through trials and tribulations, we must remember that God is in control and he has us hidden for the perfect day of our revelation. Let us then be more thankful! When death, sickness or war comes, let us remember who bought us, who protects us, who hides us, and who is in control of us.

How does it feel to know that you are chosen by God?

How can you show thankfulness to God in your day to day life?

Twenty Nine

The Parable of Unleavened Bread

Matthew 13:33

Summary: Sin has entered God's kingdom and has attempted to corrupt the perfect plan of our heavenly father. But as he has complete control, he will allow sin to take its natural course. And when the perfect time of completion is reached, God will destroy the power of sin. Until that time, he will reshape and rework his creation to the perfect purpose that he has had from the beginning.

This parable compares the kingdom of heaven to yeast that a woman takes and adds to a large amount of flour. First let us consider the significance of yeast. Yeast is a powerful substance that when added to flour makes the dough double or triple in size. My family has a tradition of baking bread so I will use this experience to step through the process of using yeast. It always amazes me that when I mix the dough it is about the size of a grapefruit, and when I return to it in about an hour, its size doubles to that of a watermelon. The amount of dough mixed in our home is to feed six people for a week. Imagine how large the dough would be if it was measured to feed over a hundred people? Now take this image and visualize something even greater: the flour being as large as all the generations that have ever existed. In this parable, the large amount of flour represents all of God's children, from the generations that have passed, to those alive today, to the generations that are yet to come- an amount we are unable to number. The yeast represents sin which was dropped into our existence by Satan, who first sinned. This sin continues to move and dwell among us, and will continually affect all of us until the appointed time of completion is reached.

Let us now consider the next step in making yeast bread to see what God has planned. The kneaded dough is then covered and set aside to rise for about an hour. Two things can happen. The dough could be set aside for too long. In this case it will keep rising until it thins out to the point where it bursts apart, and the whole batch is destroyed. Or, as is the correct way, the baker could return to the dough in perfect timing, stop the process of the yeast by deflating the dough, and rework and shape it into desirable pieces. In the same way, God reshapes us into the perfect image that he has planned for us. You cannot stem the work of the yeast too soon or too late, or it will lead to a damaged product. In the same token, our creator knows that the time to stop the works of sin must be perfect in order for his finished product to be perfect. We must therefore rest in the faith that his will for us is perfect and without flaw.

What is stopping you from giving God full control over your life?

Thirty

The Parable of the Unmerciful Servant

Matthew 18:21-35

Summary: In God's kingdom, forgiveness is key! We are not to consider ourselves as higher or better than any of God's other creation. We must remember at all times, that we are at the mercy of God, who freed us from the great debt that we owed for sin.

In this parable, the kingdom of heaven is compared to a king who went to settle accounts with his servants. As he was assessing each servant, it was time for one to come to him who owed him ten thousand talents. This servant was not able to pay the debt, so the king commanded that he, his wife, his children and all that he had must be sold so that the payment can be made. But the servant, hearing this, was devastated that everything he had was about to be taken away from him. He was so desperate that he began to worship the king and to beg him to wait a little longer for payment. "Then the lord of that servant was moved with compassion, and loosed him, and forgave him the debt" (Matthew 18:27).

I can imagine how relieved that servant felt when he realized that the threat that his family could be taken away and sold was no longer there.

But there is a terrible twist to this story. This same servant, who was just on the verge of losing everything that he had, went out and found one of his fellow servants, who owed him an hundred pence. We are told that he "laid hands on him, and took him by the throat, saying, Pay me that thou owest" (18:28). He insisted on payment even though his fellow servant fell down at his feet, begged him to have patience with him, and promised that he will pay back everything. The first servant which was pardoned by his master, would not do the same for his fellow servant, but had him put in prison until he would be able to repay the debt. The other servants who witnessed this went and told the king what happened. The king said to him, "O thou wicked servant, I forgave thee all that debt, because thou desiredst me: Shouldest not thou also have had compassion on thy fellow servant, even as I had pity on thee?" (18:32-33). The story continues that the king was very angry and delivered him to tormentors until he should pay all that was due to him. Jesus ended his story by telling his disciples that in the same way, "shall my father do also unto you, if ye from your hearts forgive not everyone his brother their trespasses" (18:35). Jesus used this story to teach us that we must show mercy on others since mercy is shown to us.

We need to be careful how we hold grudges and demand retribution from our neighbors because we are all in debt to God for the many sins that we have been pardoned. No one living on Earth is immune from sin, because we all live in close proximity to the 'tares' that have been planted in our midst. We are here because our creator looked down upon us with mercy and gave us a second chance. Just as he continues to forgive us, we must forgive others.

Is there anyone who you have not truly forgiven (from your heart)?

Why is it difficult for you to forgive these persons?

Ask God to show you what lessons he wants you to learn because of these people's actions.

Thirty One

THE PARABLE OF THE FOOLISH AND WISE

VIRGINS

MATTHEW 25:1-13

Summary: There will be a great marriage in the Kingdom one day, which all of creation prepares for, and those who will be taken in marriage to the Prince of Peace will have persevered, will be prepared, and will be equipped to inherit the greatest reward of all times: perfect bliss in union with God, for eternity.

The tense used in this parable tells us that Jesus was speaking again of a time that was to come. It begins, "Then shall the kingdom of heaven be likened unto ten virgins, which took their lamps, and went forth to meet the bridegroom" (Matthew 25:1). The story continues that five of the virgins were wise and five of them were foolish. They all took their lamps and waited in preparation of the coming of the bridegroom. The wise ones took oil with their lamps, while the foolish ones took no oil with them. They were waiting a very long time and the bridegroom still did not come. All of the virgins fell asleep. At midnight there was great excitement as it was announced that the bridegroom was finally coming. Everyone got ready to meet him, and the virgins all arose and trimmed their lamps.

The foolish virgins asked the wise ones for oil, since they did not bring along any extra oil. "But the wise answered, saying, Not so; lest there be not enough for us and you: but go ye rather to them that sell, and buy for yourselves" (Matthew 25:9). At this last minute, while the bridegroom was already in their midst, the foolish virgins left to buy oil for their lamps. The story goes that the virgins who were prepared and waiting went in with the bridegroom to the marriage and the door was shut. "Afterward came also the other virgins, saying, Lord, Lord, open to us" but he answered, "Verily I say unto you, I know you not" (25:11, 12). God's children, who he says know him, are also known by him. The people who are not his are not known by him. It is that simple. As such, he already has it planned that those who refuse to know him will not inherit his kingdom. We who are his will obey him and wait patiently for his promise of the return of Jesus Christ, because of our faith. Those who are not his will not believe, and will lose hope and fall away.

We are assured that as God's children we will hear his call and know exactly what we need to do to prepare for our bridegroom. Like the five wise virgins, the true church will rest in unwavering hope of eternal life through Jesus Christ. We will not take life for granted. And even though we'll get tired sometimes and need to rest a while, we will be alert and ready when the bridegroom's trumpet is blown. This is the promise that we must hold on to until we see Christ face to face. Jesus warns, "Watch therefore, for ye know neither the day nor the hour wherein the Son of man cometh" (25:13). The five wise virgins did not just wait, but waited in abundance! This story tells us that we must not idly wait, or ration our faith and our resources as if we can predict how soon or how late Christ will return. We might be few, but we must be filled with faith, wisdom and expectation! When that day comes will our hard work, good fight, and strong faith stand the test of time? Those who keep themselves pure and committed to him, and expectedly prepare for his arrival, will receive the crown of everlasting life. Therefore, in our dealings, our battles, and our service, we must practice the wisdom of the five wise virgins.

Spend some time praying and asking God to show you how **he** wants you to serve him, then answer the questions below.

How can you serve God better in your home?

What attitudes can you develop at your place of work to show that the love and wisdom of God govern your life?

How can you be more faithful serving God at your church?

How can you be more faithful living for God while you are having fun?

Thirty Two

THE PARABLE OF THE SERVANTS AND THE

TALENTS

MATTHEW 25:14-30

Summary- No one knows when Jesus will come back, but we are here as his church (his bride), and servants in the kingdom of God; whoever is found to be faithful in the work, humble in the walk, and righteous beyond reproof, will be given the greatest reward of all time- eternal life in heaven with Christ.

*E*ven though this parable paints a picture of what is happening currently in our lives, it is also futuristic, in that it describes what is yet to come in God's kingdom. It begins: "The kingdom of heaven is as a man traveling into a far country, who called his own servants, and delivered unto them his goods" (Matthew 25:14). He was very thoughtful in what he gave to each servant, "And unto one he gave five talents, to another two, and to another one; to every man according to his several ability; and straightway took his journey" (25:15).

You may wonder what a talent is. As you read further you will see that a talent is a form of money. It is interesting to see what the servants did with the talents that were given to them. All but one of the servants went and traded, and did business that doubled what was given to them by their master. The one who was given one talent went and dug a hole and buried it. The story continues that after a long time the master of those servants returned and asked them to tell what they did with his money. The two servants who doubled their master's money came and gave him an account of their increase. To both of them, he responded, "Well done, thou good and faithful servant: thou hast been faithful over a few things, I will make thee ruler over many things: enter thou into the joy of thy lord" (25:23). However the third servant told his master,

"Lord, I knew thee that thou art an hard man, reaping where thou hast not sown, and gathering where thou hast not strawed: And I was afraid, and went and hid thy talent in the earth: lo, there thou hast that is thine" (Matthew 25:24-25).

His lord responded, "Thou wicked and slothful servant, thou knewest that I reap where I sowed not, and gather where I have not strawed: Thou oughtest therefore to have put my money to the exchangers, and then at my coming I should have received mine own with usury" (25:26-27). The rich man then had the one talent taken from that servant and given to the one that had ten. He then continued to instruct the servants: "For unto every one that hath shall be given, and he shall have abundance: but from him that hath not shall be taken away even that which he hath. And cast ye the unprofitable servant into outer darkness: there shall be weeping and gnashing of teeth" (25:29-30). This parable is explained here very simply and anyone who has eyes to see, and ears to hear will understand the simple message.

As mentioned at the beginning of this chapter, Jesus told these parables in context to what his disciples asked, or in connection to what they were experiencing at the time. Jesus used these short stories, which could easily be remembered, to paint a picture of who we are, whose we are and what God expects from us in his kingdom. Do not take these stories lightly and think that they were random stories that Jesus made up because he had nothing better to talk about. They are heavily coded with information that can help us find our way back to God. I have done my best to share what he has laid on my heart, but please don't stop here. Pray that he inspires you with a personal revelation of what they mean. Then make it your life's duty to practice the principles that these parables teach so that you will stay on the straight and narrow path that leads us back home.

Use the space below to list the people, abilities and assets that God has placed in your life. Remember every day to thank him for these resources.

Thirty Three

THE CALL- PART ONE

"O the depth of the riches both of the wisdom and knowledge of God! how unsearchable are his judgments, and his ways past finding out! For who hath known the mind of the Lord? or who hath been his counsellor? Or who hath first given to him, and it shall be recompensed unto him again? For of him, and through him, and to him, are all things: to whom be glory forever. Amen"
— (ROMANS 11:33-36).

As creations, we each have a special purpose. This purpose is our divine calling. We are given a set of skills that makes each of us perfect for the work which God has called us to do. But many live in hopelessness, believing that there is no importance to their lives. At specific times, which vary from person to person, God calls us to do a work for him. Since he is not bound by time or space, he has planned before we were born all that he wanted us to do. We have some degree of freewill as part of his framework, but there is a set pattern that was laid out before time began, which will be accomplished. God's Word states, "In whom also we have obtained an inheritance, being predestinated according to the purpose of him who worketh all things after the counsel of his own will:" (Ephesians 1:11). We can conclude from this passage that there are also some who God did not foreknow and who will never accept him as Lord because they are not his children. The obvious question is: how God could be sovereign but not know some things? It is not the purpose of this book to reveal all that this means. Just know that all of his children were known prior to their existence here on Earth, and this is never to be taken lightly. As a child of the Most High God, hold on tight to this truth and know that as his child, you are under his control no matter how terrible your situations may seem.

In reverence we must ask him to guide our every thought, word and action. We must place all of our confidence and trust in him, instead of putting our hopes in the people and things in our lives. It is his law that must govern our lives! Our creator, being all knowing and all powerful, can do anything he wants to, and he always takes time to study our growth and level of submission to him. Not being bound by time, he sees the whole, while we see in part. He can call us at the age of a child, as an adult, or when we are very old for the different works that he needs us to do.

Our calling can be for a purpose that we might least expect, because God sees what we cannot see. Circumstances will happen and people will show up with the needed resources to propel us into the chosen direction of our calling. But once again, we have some amount of choice in how we will respond to what God places in our lives. For us to be perfect for our calling, we are born at just the right time, given a specific set of family members, and allowed a perfect set of experiences to adequately prepare us. This is why the existence of each one of us is a scientific miracle. Seeing how infinitely amazing we each were created should be enough to bring us to complete worship of God and a greater respect for ourselves as individual souls.

There are many stories in the Bible which give examples about how people respond to being called. As shown by the examples of these men and women, God sees everyone before we were born. He knew what was to be found in each of us, and determined what would be best for us. He therefore calls us at times that would make each soul fit in perfectly with the rest of creation. We were given the power to choose how we will respond to his call, but the consequences that result always fit into his divine order. Many abuse this privilege of choice and choose their own way. The stories in the Bible show that if we do not let God govern our lives, and continue in our disobedience, we will eventually pay the price with our own souls. He has seen all of the generations of man before time began. Based on what he saw he decided to call many. At the end of time, after all has been done to reach and teach us, few will be chosen. Will you be one of the few chosen to live in eternal peace and joy with our savior? Or will you be rejected like some of the people from Jesus' parables?

Evidence that God knows the whole story of creation is seen throughout scripture. "For now we see through a glass, darkly; but then face to face: now I know in part; but then shall I know even as also I am known" (1 Corinthians 13:12). Our creator's intimate knowledge of us is often confusing to grasp because we often put him in a box based on what we have been taught. Even though he sees our condition, he still strives to shape us into an acceptable image of righteousness.

God is love and everything he does is done because of his love for his children. Here is a passage that expresses the all-encompassing love that he has for us. "For I am persuaded, that neither death, nor life, nor angels, nor principalities, nor powers, nor things present, nor things to come, Nor height, nor depth, nor any other creature, shall be able to separate us from the love of God, which is in Christ Jesus our Lord" (Romans 8:38). Our heavenly father's love determines everything about our life story. He knows who his children are, he sees what we are capable of, and as a result he keeps watch over us. We are never alone!

We have all been called here to Earth to build up God's kingdom. We are called to learn, grow, believe, live, love, and to worship him. And no matter what our specific calling is, our lives should demonstrate a commitment to following God's law.

What do you feel is the main purpose of your life? (Ask God to show you what it is.)

What is stopping you from doing what God wants you to do?

What steps can you take today to answer God's call?

Thirty Four

THE CALL- PART TWO

Though I speak with the tongues of men and of angels, and have not charity, I am become as sounding brass, or a tinkling cymbal. And though I have the gift of prophecy, and understand all mysteries, and all knowledge; and though I have all faith, so that I could remove mountains, and have not charity, I am nothing. And though I bestow all my goods to feed the poor, and though I give my body to be burned, and have not charity, it profiteth me nothing. Charity suffereth long, and is kind; charity envieth not; charity vaunteth not itself, is not puffed up, Doth not behave itself unseemly, seeketh not her own, is not easily provoked, thinketh no evil; Rejoiceth not in iniquity, but rejoiceth in the truth;

— (1 CORINTHIANS 13:1-6).

We read in the previous chapters that we are each uniquely equipped with specific abilities and resources that make each of us a perfect unit for the building and maintenance of God's kingdom. We also learned that God calls us at different times into this life to do different things based on his perfect will. Now let us examine how we are prepared to do his work. The above verse shows us that it is through his divine love that he refines us to perfection so that we will be able to perform to his standards. Our creator could have wired us to robotically function within his love, just like he has given us many other abilities, but forcing us to love him would not be true love. This passage shows us that if we have no charity or agape love our work will be found lacking, no matter how talented or dedicated we are. As a result, we are instructed on how to love God and how to love as he loves, so that we will be prepared for eternal life.

Here our heavenly father is telling us that if we do not have love for the people that he has placed in our lives, our gifts and our calling will be ineffective to the building up of his kingdom. This is because his divine love is the connection which causes all of creation to function in harmony. Everything and everyone responds to love because the whole of creation was created by God, who is love. Love is therefore the divine language of all of creation. Imagine someone sitting in an interview to be considered for the position of a Principal. There is a panel of high level administrators sitting around him at a conference table. They fire away questions about his life experiences, education, beliefs and about his knowledge of teaching children. This is done so that the interviewers can get a sense of if he loves working with children and adults and can handle the difficulties that will arise if he is hired as a principal. As they listen to his answers, they analyze his level of sincerity. Anyone being considered for a job goes through a similar experience as the one just described because the persons responsible for hiring don't just want qualified and highly skilled workers, but 'real people' who truly love the work. Most of the questions asked at an interview are therefore directed at our emotions to test the level of our love. Someone may be highly skilled and very knowledgeable of the field, but does that person have a true passion for the work at hand? It is this true love for the work that will matter most in times of hardship. God, being our creator, knows all of this better than we do. So in judging us he always looks at the quality of our love.

Why is love so important in doing the work that God calls us to do? It is when we learn to love like he loves that we become more like his image. In this way we can truly empathize with the needy and intercede for those in danger, instead of being paralyzed by fear in the wake of a disaster. Through the perfect love of God, our fear becomes faith, and this gives us the courage to stand up to any struggle (1 John 4:18). Unless it is a fear that would drive us to obey God, fear is not truth. The world today is driven by self-destructive fear, so I urge you today to let your life be driven by faith, hope and love as you look toward our hope of everlasting life in heaven.

The love that Jesus showed when he suffered and died for us reveals the full maturity of love that we are talking about here. God's experience as man (through Jesus) made him able to empathize with man's activities here on Earth. Ask yourself this, how could someone save another if the savior has no knowledge of the experiences of the person that he is trying to save? In layman's terms, how could a lawyer defend someone without knowing the intimate details of that person's life? How can someone rescue a drowning person if he himself cannot swim? And how can a doctor perform a heart surgery if he has not carefully studied the organ or the tools that must be used? In the same way, God became familiar with death and with the fallen state of man through Jesus Christ.

Let us shift perspectives now to our own lives. Our creator allows challenges of all levels to come into our lives to teach us how to persevere, how to be patient, and how to be humble. This all boils down to perfecting our love, for it is when we are doing these things that we are made perfect in love. And as our love becomes more like Christ, we develop into the image that God first intended for us when he created us. We become more humble with our possessions and positions! Our entire existence (the gifts we are given at conception, our physical bodies, our assets, and the people that come into our lives) is all to teach us this perfect love of our creator.

You may have experienced tragedies in your childhood or adulthood. You may be going through something really devastating right now, like a terminal illness or the death of a loved one. You may be challenged at your job or at school. Whatever you are going through, know that you can ask God to show you that situation through the eyes of love. His love shows up, and his power is manifested greatly, in hard times. What you are going through right now can strengthen you in your areas of spiritual weakness or prepare you for a work in the future, where you will need the experiences that this situation will give you.

"Are you showing your love toward me by allowing this situation into my life, because there is some aspect of my soul that needs to grow?" "Is this situation to change the direction of my life and take me down a better path?" "Is this what you planned for my loved one even before time began?" When we are burdened with despair, these are the questions that our souls pour out to God. But many times we turn and walk away from him before he gives us an answer because of fear or resentment. He answers us when we sincerely ask and patiently wait for an answer. Rest assured knowing that everything that happens to you is for your best interest.

If you need more information on how God works on our souls, I urge you to stop here and **try** to read the eighth chapter of the book of Romans completely. It is a very tough read, but even if you only get through one verse you will walk away with a greater respect of our creator. Many times when we experience hardship, we grieve or we rebuke the devil. We should first talk to our heavenly father, the absolute supreme, Most High God. We must humbly approach him and patiently wait until he answers us. Waiting is very important because many times we pray, then in impatience we answer our own prayers through our own reasoning. While we wait for an answer we need to deliberately choose to be open minded, because his answers will often surprise us. If we try to predict the answer, it might be right in front of us and we will totally miss it. Many believe that prayer is us just talking to God, but as I said before, it is both talking and listening! The goal is to get to the point where you listen to him more than you ask for things. Today, start training yourself to listen with open-mindedness, and let the Holy Spirit of God speak to you. Remember that what his Spirit tells you will always line up with truth because God is of order and his principles do not contradict one another.

Revisit the times that you have set for your alone time with God, and list what changes you would like to make.

Do you have a prayer journal? If not, start one here. Use the space below to write down the needs that you would like God to answer. Revisit your list each week, or each month, and check off answered prayers.

Thirty Five

THE CALL- PART THREE

"For I know the thoughts that I think toward you, saith the LORD, thoughts of peace, and not of evil, to give you an expected end. Then shall ye call upon me, and ye shall go and pray unto me, and I will hearken unto you. And ye shall seek me, and find me, when ye shall search for me with all your heart"
— (JEREMIAH 29:11-13).

*I*n this section we will take a quick look at some people from the Bible and see how they handled their calling. As we study the lives of these men and women, let us inspect our own lives, and ask God to show us if there are any similarities or lessons to be learned.

Adam

Adam was called to care for Earth and to subdue it along with the other creatures that lived on it. Adam did what God called him to do until he was persuaded by his wife, Eve, to eat from the forbidden tree. His choice in Eden teaches us that even the best and most knowledgeable of us can be persuaded to disobey God. All it takes is a friend who we believe in and trust, and we will, for a moment, take our focus off of his commands. We can learn from this that the Word of God and the work that he calls us to do should be more important to us than anyone else in our lives, including our spouse. His Word must be so much a part of us that everything we think, say or do should take us back to scripture. It is written, "Man cannot live by bread alone but by every word that proceedeth from the mouth of God" (Matthew 4:4). We often let our resources and responsibilities take over our lives and choke out any trace of scripture from our minds. And we become confused and forgetful of what we once knew so readily.

Know that if one principle of God's truth is rejected but for a moment, a soul's growth could be set back for decades. Because of this we must be disciplined in seeking our creator's will before thinking any thought or taking action. You may have a problem. And you might develop a plan that seems like the perfect solution. No matter how solid or fool-proof that plan seems to you, DO NOT act on it until you ask God about it and you know for sure that he gives you liberty to act. My church's Youth Director once made a statement that was eye opening and taught me to be more careful when making plans. He said, "If your good is not the good that God has intended for you to do, then it is not good for you to do it." You may think that this is just an opinion and that our free will gives us the power to go against God's plans. But the Word of God makes it clear that "except the LORD build the house, they labour in vain that build it: except the LORD keep the city, the watchman waketh *but* in vain" (Psalm 127:1). As Adam's disobedience shows us, no matter how legitimate our motives may be, God's commandments must always be our first priority.

If you read Chapter three of the book of Genesis you will see that several curses were placed on Adam and Eve, and on all of the generations of man because of their sin of disobedience. We, the offspring of Adam and Eve, are living under these curses 'till today. I strongly urge you to read this chapter in Genesis to verify this. But the good news, my brothers and sisters, is that the curses can be lifted if we each repent and turn our lives over to God! One of the curses is that the man will have dominion over his wife. This was not the original plan because Adam and Eve were meant to function as compliments of each other (co-laborers). This would explain why Adam listened to Eve. Today, men sometimes fight just the mere idea of listening to their wives, and sometimes even laud their authority over them. This was not the original plan. We need to constantly pray and ask God for wisdom in our actions. We can individually ask him to teach us how to live with our spouse the way he intended, instead of accepting the curses brought on by our ancestors. That is why we are here: to individually get the chance to choose to be free from the curses caused by Adam and his wife!

Is there someone in your life who can be your accountability partner to remind you to keep your focus on God?

How would you rate or describe your personal Bible study/ prayer life?

What are some steps that you could take to improve your personal Bible study/ prayer life?

Eve

Eve was created to be Adam's helper and companion. We are told that when she was created, God found that she was the perfect match for Adam; she was given all that she needed to be his helper in every way. But Eve was tempted by Satan to disobey God. Her conversation with Satan shows us the troubles that come when we entertain sin, or try to reason with temptations to sin, instead of being totally focused on God's commands. It is when we entertain the thought that we can obey him partially that we fall prey to temptation. We must never try to reason with sinful thoughts, but just remain completely focused on what the Word says in every moment!

Why shouldn't we reason with sin? This is never to be done because our enemy, the spiritual beings which roam this world, are experts in deception. Their father, Satan, created it, therefore, we are no match for them and will never be able to find their schemes wanting. Their goal is to never let you find out that they are real, or a threat. If you did, you would run to God in fear. So they work by keeping us reasoning, while they pull us further and further away from God's protection. As you are surrounded by more and more confusion, it is you who will make the choice to sin. The Word of God is the only weapon that vanquishes their lies and temptations.

I often wonder why Eve even had time to reason with Satan? I notice that the world keeps women distracted with the same lie that Eve was told, that "there is something else out there to make you wiser, happier and prettier". Have you ever taken the time to wonder why? A woman was created perfectly to compliment a man, yet she is constantly pushed to make alterations upon herself.

The ability to birth children, the woman's intuitive and nurturing abilities, and her desire to see the men in her life grow to their highest potentials are some of the many traits that were given to the woman to help the man. Because of these nurturing traits that the woman was designed with, it is even more important that she never reasons with sin. Everything that a woman says, thinks or does MUST be done only after consulting God and being sure that the directions she is about to follow match his divine principles of truth. As a result of this great need for Godly wisdom, a woman's closest asset and companion must be the Word of God.

It is essential that both men and women live a life of total dependency on God's Word. But I notice from experience and from reading scripture that men listen to women, and many women have destroyed the lives of men because they gave them advice outside of the Word of God. Another thing I observed is that many women give advice without first praying and seeking God's will because of their emotional and intuitive traits. A woman must never give her children, her husband, or anyone else any advice without first praying to God about it and waiting for liberty to speak. I am stressing the need to seek God first because many times ladies have given advice from the Word of God that seemed right, but they never consulted God first. The results have been devastating.

My point here is that the enemy knows the special touch that God made the woman with, and he uses it against her and against humanity as a whole. So let us all remember to keep God's words close and seek his will at all times.

Another lesson that we can learn from Eve is that we must make sure we are not *hanging out* with sinners. As we learned before, we all sin. So "*sinners*" here refers to those who go about life with the deliberate intention to disobey God. They simply do not care about the consequences of their actions. The passage that reinforces the truth that we should watch the company we keep is below: "Blessed is the man that walketh not in the counsel of the ungodly, nor standeth in the way of sinners, nor sitteth in the seat of the scornful" (Psalm 1:1). We must, at all cost, avoid the paths of those who willfully and nonchalantly sin, because we are usually not strong enough to resist the temptations of our peers. We so want to fit in that we compromise because of the pressures we feel. If we do choose to stay out of the company of sinners, we must do something instead: be busy and preoccupied with serving God and making him pleased!

All of the above is true for everyone, but women especially have to be deliberate and wise in making decisions for their families because many times the men are not present. Many men have been carried away from their walk with God, and removed from their position in their households, as they are taken by the temptations of this world. It is not easy being a woman today because the burdens of the family are most often carried by her. But God is all-powerful and there is nothing that is too difficult for him to do. So whether you are a man or a woman, learn from the temptations of Eve and let God have total dominion over your life.

How can you be more busy serving God in the home?

How can you be more busy serving God at your place of worship?

How can you be more busy serving God at work?

How can you be more busy serving God in your time of leisure/ relaxation?

Noah

Noah was found to be righteous in God's eyes, while everyone else around him were engaging in sins which were found to be abominable. God knew that the only way to eradicate the effects of what they were doing was to flood Earth entirely. But he did not just condemn Noah's generation; he gave them about a hundred years to repent and turn away from their sins (it took that long for Noah to build the arc). After all that time, they still did not change from their wicked ways. I can imagine how lonely and foolish Noah felt as he tried to explain that rain was going to fall and flood Earth completely, when the people of his time never experienced rain before. I could imagine how difficult it was for him to build something that he had never built before, and trust that it was going to be just as God instructed.

A century later, the rain came just as he said it would. Noah, his family, and a sample of all of the species of land animals were saved on the ark, while everyone else was destroyed by that flood.

The more we try to obey and put our faith in God, the more people will rebuke and persecute us. It is then that we must persevere and be strong in his promises. Noah's story also teaches that there is power in one. It is the unwavering faith of one man (Noah) that gave all of us the ability to be alive today. We each now have a choice of whether we will be in the unrighteous majority as the doomed people of Noah's time, or one of the righteous minority who will be saved. Remember what we learned before that many are called but few are chosen (Matthew 22:14). If you are being laughed at or treated badly because you believe that there is coming another apocalypse, remember the flood, and like Noah, keep building your faith. If you are discouraged because your righteousness takes you out of the 'party scene', be assured that that is what God expects from you, and that eternal life in glory will be your reward. Him judging your life as righteous is the only judgement that matters.

Take some time to list the passages of scripture that give you strength in the space below. (You may choose from what is given in this book or from other sources. Finding them directly from the Bible is always best). Write each of your favorite verses on index cards and keep them in your purse or wallet. It helps to have God's words at the ready to help, especially in times of decision making or spiritual attack.

Rahab

Many of us know Rahab as the prostitute of Jericho who helped the Israelites to attack and conquer her town. She could have wallowed away in fear as the other people of Jericho did when they knew of the Israelites' impending attack. Instead, she thought of a way to befriend the Israelites. Instead of maintaining loyalty to her community, she changed loyalties to the Most High God for her safety and that of her family. Rahab obeyed the directions that the Israelite spies gave her perfectly, and because of her complete obedience in a difficult situation, she and her family were saved. We can learn from Rahab to obey directions precisely when we are given them from God's messengers. We can also learn that being his friend has greater benefits than being a friend of this world. Each soul's first priority should be to become a greater friend of God than a friend of anyone else. We must make time to study how he has saved others, and desire that he saves us as well.

Make a list of all of the things in your life that you value.

Are you putting these things before God?

Jonah

Jonah is the runaway prophet who had to encounter some very cat-astrophic situations in his life before he could obey God. He did not want to go and preach a message of salvation to the Ninevites, as he was asked to. He thought that their sins were unforgiveable and did not want them to repent and evade punishment. He knew that if he prophesied to them the people would repent and be saved. We are each like Jonah when we refuse to do what God asks us to do because we think we know what is best for ourselves or for the people in our lives. We must learn from this story that our cre-ator is in control of everything, sees everything, and forgives and loves whomever he wants to.

Our life should be one of absolute obedience, doing whatever God calls us to do instead of analyzing what he tells us. We must learn to be thankful for all that we have and for all that God does, knowing that he has created all things and knows us best. Our faith must always take precedence over our reasoning. And as Jonah learned, let us also realize that no one can hide from God. He used a whale to swallow Jonah up and rescue him from his suicide at-tempt as he jumped into the sea to get away from God's calling. No matter how difficult God's instructions may be, and no matter how undeserving the people who we are called to serve may seem in our eyes, we MUST obey him. From experience, I can tell you that the faster you obey God, the easier obeying him gets, while the more you disobey him, the harsher his instructions get.

As a side note, let me add that there will be rare cases where God will ask you to do something difficult, and when he sees that you have made up your mind to obey, he will tell you not to do it anymore. When this happens, you will fall more deeply in love with our heavenly father, and you will be relieved that that *difficult thing* was taken from you. But you will be very encouraged because you knew that you had settled in your heart to do that work. God does not do this because he *changes his mind*; he does things like this to test our growth, to show us what areas still need work, and to reveal his mercy and grace!

This being said, never approach a task that God gave you thinking that he might not make you go through with it. He is never expecting to find partial faith in us, and he might just let you go through with that thing. Let us learn from Jonah that our minds can never predict what God is going to do, no matter how righteous we may think we are.

Has God ever asked you to be kind to someone who was unkind to you? Did you obey? Explain what happened.

Jesus

Jesus entered time and gave us the means by which we can be reconciled back to God. There is great controversy about what language he spoke, what he looked like, and what people called him when he lived on Earth. I believe that these concerns will all be resolved one day when all is revealed. "Therefore judge nothing before the time, until the Lord comes, who both will bring to light the hidden things of darkness, and will make manifest the counsels of the hearts: and then shall every man have praise of God" (1 Corinthians 4:5). It does not matter what Jesus looked like or what language he spoke, just like it does not matter what the other men and women of scripture looked like. All that matters is that we do not worship any image of these people and we learn the lessons that they have been called here to teach us.

Jesus shows us the way back home. He shows us the spiritual meaning of the law. Finally, he shows us how fulfilled and how powerful we each could be if we submit every part of ourselves to God. Imagine the things we would be able to do if we live, love and lift God up like Jesus did (and still does). We must determine today to be more and more like Jesus.

How can you obey God more like Jesus?

How can you have more faith like Jesus?

How can you love more like Jesus?

How can you serve more like Jesus?

How can you worship more like Jesus?

Mary Magdalene

Mary Magdalene first met Jesus as she was about to be stoned by a mob for adultery. He did not follow the crowd's request, but told them that whoever is among them that never sinned should throw the first stone at her. No one did, and Mary's life was saved that day. Mary became one of Jesus' most faithful followers and friends, and she was one of the first to see him when he resurrected. I learned from Mary Magdalene's story that no matter what you have done in your life, you can make up your mind to change and recommit your life back to God. It is never too late for even the most hardened sinners if they confess their sins and truly repent. You could be demon possessed, engaged in any of the forms of sexual perversion, or a murderer; if you reach out to God sincerely and tell him that you want to change your wicked ways (repent), he will transform you into an image of righteousness that is pure beyond reproach. He sees all of his children the same: as sinners in need of his mercy and grace. But our story does not have to stop where he finds us.

Never lose hope in God's abilities to save and to transform! Never let others tell you that your circumstances can't change. And when God takes you out of a pit, thank him and don't look back. Anything that causes you to look back (other than God's Holy Spirit) is an attack from the enemy. Put on your armor and invoke the Word of God daily to fight your way out of your battles. Believe that God's promises are true, and help others who are in a pit. When you help others you accept and strengthen your own victory! When you don't help others, thinking that you have your own set of issues to work out, you actually give these "issues" the power to put you in bondage again. So I say to you: know the Word, use the Word, dare to GROW UP in your faith, and help somebody!

What pit (a way of life or situation that you know is against God's law) are you in that you need someone to rescue you from? Explain in detail.

What is stopping you from turning that situation over to God?

Ask our heavenly father to give you the strength to pray, the right words to say, and the faith to believe that he can deliver you, not later, but today!

Thirty Six

The Call- Part Four

"Your eyes saw my unformed body. All the days ordained for me were written in your book before one of them came to be"
— (Psalm 139:16).

*I*magine a craft shop with all kinds of amazing creations. The owner is an artist whose talent is unmatched by any other person in the world. His shop has all kinds of colorful crafts, vases, rugs, and musical instruments of every kind. The shelves are neatly labeled and carefully stacked, and every aisle is comfortable to walk through. Imagine also that this craft shop is the size of Earth. Now think for a moment what it would be like if this artist could create things by simply speaking them into existence. How alike are his different creations? I can imagine rows of shelves of unique creations that I've never seen before, all different from each other in size, shape, color and style. This is the same unique way that our creator has made each and every one of us.

Every artist has a masterpiece, and man is God's masterpiece! He did not just call us forth with his Word, but he also formed bodies from the Earth to house us. Because we are each an individual soul in his masterpiece collection, each one of us is designed for a specific purpose! Stop trying to be like others, because all that you could ever be is YOU! Stop letting people make you fit into the image that their limited minds think of you. Today, be thankful for your uniqueness and start asking God to reveal your special purpose (your calling).

Every time I read the opening verse of this chapter I am overwhelmed with thankfulness. We, God's children, did not just appear from out of nowhere. We were carefully and lovingly formed, and all of our days were planned out for us. I wondered for a long time how I came into being from nothing, as many scientific theories suggest. How is it that before the sperm and the egg connected in my mother's fallopian tube I did not exist? Think of how many sperms were lost before the one that fertilized your egg came to be. Then imagine how many eggs were lost during your mother's menstrual cycles before the egg which you were going to be formed in showed up on the scene. Each of God's children was first conceived in his mind before he formed us. We did not appear here from nowhere! We came from somewhere. A place where even though we do not know, he knows (Psalm 139:15). It is comforting to know that someone knows me that thoroughly. But it does not stop there. There are many instances in scripture where we see that God even knows his children by name. This lets us know that he wants to have a personal relationship with each one of us, and that we were each created for a unique purpose. So let us remember always that we belong to someone: our unchangeable heavenly father, the Most High God.

He formed us, then placed us in the family, to live in the culture, and to have the experiences which he knew would be perfect for making us who he wanted us to become. He is now preparing us so that we will each be best-suited for the plans that he has for us today, and for the destination that he has prepared for us in the future. If we follow this line of reasoning, we will be able to see life differently. We will see that everything that we have is a special asset to make the real us a wonderful masterpiece. We are a work in progress, affected by the choices we make. Will we choose to let God finish his perfect work in us by surrendering our thoughts, our will and our desires to him? Or will we choose to be rebellious and swim against the tides as Jonah did, kick against the pricks as Paul did, or by wrestling with God as many still choose to do today? Fighting his plans will cause us to experience hell right here on Earth. But this hell is a shadow of the hell that is prepared for all those who will go to their graves refusing the ultimate gift, which is eternal life in heaven.

Let us look a little deeper at three unique gifts God gives us when he calls us into this world. They are our family, our culture and our experiences. The faithful day of your physical conception, one of your father's sperms pierced your mother's egg, and the two bodies became one. The egg was fertilized, and you were given the gift of two families: your mother's family and your father's family. You inherited these two families' history, physical and non-physical traits. These non-physical traits include the emotional, social and mental traits which you cannot always see with your naked eyes, but are there. Even though you cannot see all of these messages from your ancestors, they manifest as you grow from an object which cannot be seen with the naked eyes to that baby that leaves the womb on your birthday. And they continue to shape your unique personality as you grow. I am not saying that adoptive parents do not count as a gift from God. He gives each of us the family that he knows will fulfil his purpose for us. But experienced adoptive parents can attest to the fact that there comes a time when the adopted child asks about the biological parents.

This desire to connect with the "blood line" is there and is necessary for the child to see what lessons need to be learned or unlearned in life. When we hate our families, or reject family members, we choose to step out of God's will in our minds, and limit the perfect healing, learning and maturing process of our own soul. Instead, we must release these members for God to judge them accordingly. We must then, with caution and after seeking his will, try to find out more about the ways of our own biological parents. It is necessary that we study their actions of the past andpresent and see what the consequences of those actions are. A person who runs from his/her family will find life very confusing and will feel disconnected until he/she somehow reconnects with at least one member of the family and take the time to study that family's history.

When we tap into our family's background and we analyze the strengths and the weaknesses therein, we must then ask God to show us what to do with this information. Miracles happen when we do this! We see where each family member fits and why we were born into this family. We see which of our ancestors' mistakes we are repeating. God will show us what needs continued work and what traits are already refined.

If you have an adopted child, the life experiences that your family gives to the child is exactly what that soul needs in order to grow as God wants it to. Sometimes it might not be wise to make contact with the biological family, because of legal issues. However, if you have the ability to have this child contact or learn about his biological family from a distance, seek God's approval first and then do what he says. If it is his will that the child does not contact the biological family, all of that child's needs will be met by you, the new parents. Please do not take from this that adopted children cannot be all that God wants them to be if they never meet their biological parents. We have read in this book time and again that if we seek God he will make a way even where there seems to be no way. The main lesson to be learned here about families is that getting to know members of one's biological family makes it very easy for us to see our own personal strengths and weaknesses, while rejecting and refusing to study one's family may lead to a delay in the soul's growth.

The gift of the family that we each were born into is divine, and no matter how messed up we think our family might be, that first core group from which we are *hatched* cannot be replaced. It was given to us by God to shape us into what he needs us to be in his kingdom. Many people avoid their families for several reasons, not realizing that this will limit their own personal growth. To reject your family is to give up the most basic thing that makes you who you are. And no matter how sincere you try to be with the new people in your life, they will be able to sense that something about you doesn't add up.

See from this that you are related to your family like a puzzle piece. Even though you might feel as though you do not fit in, each person born into a family is a missing link: the perfect piece that helps the unit to fit together. God's purpose is fulfilled when family members take up their rightful position in their family's puzzle and be exactly what he has called them to be. Just like there is a perfect spot for each puzzle piece, the same way there is a perfect spot for each and every family member. The problem comes when members compete for the same spot, have an image for family members that God did not plan, or altogether refuse their own spot in the family. This is true for a 'church family' or any other group that you find yourself in.

Let me clarify that I am not saying that we should love our family members to the point of accepting their crimes or sins. The purpose of the family is for the glorification of God, and he is not in the business of letting sin go without judgement. That being said, our first calling is to help our own family to develop a closer walk with God. Each family member is given a specific assignment to help that family as a whole to know God better. One member might be the prayer warrior, who makes time to intercede for members of the family. One might be the counselor, the person who everyone goes to with personal problems and sensitive issues. One might be the fighter, the one everyone goes to when they want advice on how to deal with difficult people or situations. And in every family there is a healer, the one everybody goes to for advice when they are sick. One might be the educator, one who is able to analyze and communicate information for others to understand. A family will also have a mediator, the one who everyone goes to when there is in-fighting in the family. One might be the pacifier, to reassure everyone to be calm in times of trouble. There is also the leader of the pack, the patriarch or matriarch, who unifies the family, or who everyone flocks to for family gatherings. And don't forget the historian! Every family has someone who cares a little more about how it all fits together, and studies how the events and the personalities of the family's past affect its present circumstances.

None of these roles is more important than another, and sometimes one person has more than one roles. What is interesting is that family members recognize the traits in each other, even though the trait-holders may not see the traits in themselves. Sometimes the traits are seen but ignored by others. This rejection occurs because of jealousy, which stems from a lack of knowledge that everyone has a special part to play. This is why many families, or even church families, have broken fellowship and disjoined relationships. As a result of this in-fighting, the family struggles to progress upward because they are too busy pulling down the puzzle pieces every time there is progress. I hope that the reader will now see the importance of pulling together as a family.

Hidden in each of us is the history of thousands of years of family information. That is why every family produces the careers which its members feel naturally drawn to. A specific combination of skills is passed down from generation to generation. For example, on my father's side, there are many entrepreneurs who have a knack for doing business, and their ventures usually bring great success. My father's family is also strong in natural healing, and cleaning. You may not think that "cleaning" is special, but that's where we get it wrong; there is no skill or ability that is better or worse in God's eyes. On my mother's side, there are many talented people in the fields of health, gardening, teaching, music and hospitality. No matter what other careers are tried, my mother's relatives always seem to end up in the fields I just mentioned. At different points in my life I have pursued one or more of the above listed fields with a passion, without realizing where these skills came from. While writing this chapter, my eyes were opened to the wide array of talents that my father's and mother's families possess, which for many years went untapped. As parents, we have a responsibility to look for the traits and abilities that our children have, and to guide them in finding their calling. It is therefore important to study our families because they are a reflection of the struggles, weaknesses and strengths that we will each have in this life.

What abilities come natural to your father's family?

What abilities come natural to your mother's family?

What personality traits exist in your father's family?

What personality traits exist in your mother's family?

Thirty Seven

THE CALL- PART FIVE

"Trust in the LORD with all thine heart; and lean not unto thine own understanding. In all thy ways acknowledge him, and he shall direct thy paths"
— (PROVERBS 3:5-6).

Second to the family, culture is the next major influence on our beliefs and actions. Simply defined, culture is the way of life of a group of people. Each family has a culture. Each neighborhood has a culture. And each country has its culture. How then is culture developed? As people experience life, they come to conclusions, develop beliefs, and their will is shaped about what they like and value and how they believe things are to be done. Some of the things that we take for granted as personality traits are actually products of our cultural backgrounds: such as our beliefs, languages, holidays, religious practices, clothes, what we like to eat, and what makes us happy or angry. All of these factors, and the many others that have not been listed, help to give us an image of who we **think** we are. Ask yourself: who should be the one to tell you who you are? The answer should be the Most High God, our heavenly father. We must take the time to study our beliefs and question if they come from him or man, because much of what we believe about ourselves and our creator come from our upbringing and not necessarily from the Word. We must turn all of these things over to God and learn to focus on his Word as the foundation of our belief system.

People take great pride in their culture, and end up putting their cultural teachings above the Word of God. I have been one of those people for most of my life. I was so prideful of my Guyanese upbringing that I made judgements about everything else based on how I was raised instead of using the Word as my standard. We need to be careful with the pride that is developed as we hold on to how we were culturally trained. We must be careful because some of those beliefs are imaginations that clash with God's principles of truth. Because of this clash it becomes an uphill battle for us to work together. Instead of listening obediently to God, we filter his words through the *log* in our eyes (all of the ideas that we have developed over time which conflicts with truth). Our superstitions and what we imagine to be greater sins than others are some of the ideas that should be cast down because they contradict the true words of God. Being willing to relearn everything as a child is a huge hump that we must get over in order for us to truly grow.

We must individually make it a point to trust in God with all of our hearts and not just rely on our own understanding. Instead of coming to the table to meet God with preconceived ideas about who he is and what he wants, we must seek him with clean hands and pure hearts, willing to relearn everything as a child. This is exactly what Jesus taught. He said that unless we become as a child, we cannot enter into the kingdom of heaven (Matthew 18:3). Being the smartest person in the room does not impress our creator. This is not because he is petty or jealous of you. He created all that we are and all that we have, so why would he be jealous of our stuff? What impress God is a heart that says, "Thank you, because all I have comes from you", thoughts that ask, "What can I do for you with these abilities that you have given me?" and a will that says, "I give myself to you, take me and use me according to YOUR will!

As an International Degree major, I got many opportunities to learn about the 'strongholds' culture has on us. I studied the role culture plays in our lives in various courses of Anthropology and by living in Morocco for several months. Living in this North African country, I quickly found out that many things that I thought were right differed from what people there thought were right. For example, In Morocco it is very common for men to walk in the streets holding hands, whereas this never occurred in the culture I grew up in. By the way, the culture of men or ladies holding hands is not a sign of their sexuality in any way. They were either friends or relatives. Another example of a cultural difference is that in Morocco it is very common for everyone to go home for lunch; parents and children walk or drive home in the middle of the day to sit together and eat a freshly made meal. At the table, one meal is usually put out into a big platter and everyone eats from this one container. Before then, I never experienced this communal form of eating. Their way of taking time in the middle of the day to *break bread* as a family made an impact on my life and it reshaped my ideas about how a family ought to share a meal. There are things about every culture that line up with the Word of God. And there are many that go against it. Even though our creator knows that we will have cultural differences, he expects us to always put him above all that we value.

Our growth is hindered when we believe that it is only our family and culture that make us who we are. In our daily dealings with people, and as we interact with different cultures, we must practice these three points:

First, we are to recognize that our culture is not who God originally created us to be; it is how we were trained by our society. When we become sensitive to the actions of others, and our emotions begin to take control, we must put them back in check, knowing that living in Christ and under the full armor of God makes us a new creature. As we are told, we can do all things through Christ which strengthens us (Philippians 4:13). Secondly, we must realize that everyone around us has a culture. We are complex creations influenced by the many places where we have lived. You may share the same looks with someone else, live in the same country, grow up in the same state, and even dress the same way, but have a totally different upbringing! Many of us speak and do as we like with the people in our lives, believing that they must accept our behavior because that is who we are. Who made us the standard by which everyone else must be judged? If you truly want to reduce conflict between you and the people who are in your life, take time to ask about their culture with the sincere desire to understand them better. The third point that I would like to make is that we must let God show us what aspects of our own, and other people's cultures, are according to truth, and which ones need to be responsibly rejected. God reaches all cultures equally. However, he expects us to always seek his will in all that we think, say and do.

God knows we have many different physical and spiritual needs, but if we seek his will first, all that we truly need will be manifested into our lives (Matthew 6:33). He also shows us what values are supreme, no matter which culture we identify with (Galations 5:22-23). And he gives us the standards by which we should live with others no matter how alike or different their actions are from ours (Philippians 4:8). Today, as we think about what culture(s) we identify with, let us remember that as a child of God, our true culture is the Culture of the Holy Spirit, as clearly outlined in the three passages of scripture above.

What cultures have influenced your life? (Think of the countries, neighborhoods, places of work and worship that have influence your life.)

Thirty Eight

THE CALL- PART SIX

Trust in the LORD with all thine heart; and lean not unto thine own understanding. In all thy ways acknowledge him, and he shall direct thy paths" — (PROVERBS 3:5-6).

In addition to family and culture, our experience is the next major influence on the choices we make in life. The experiences that come into our lives are inevitably controlled by Almighty God. He sees our souls and works out experiences to encourage its growth. Our enemy is concerned with defiling our souls, and intends that we stay in confusion and ignorance. The spiritual forces among us study our strengths and weaknesses and launch their attack in the weak areas that they find. They are in our midst encouraging us to focus on negative thoughts, disbelief and fear, and push us to judge our experiences based on lies. Some of our experiences are affected by what our parents and other ancestors did before us. I must note here that it is important for parents to dig into their family's history and study the weaknesses that their relatives have struggled with. We then need to ask God to pull down every curse and break every chain of spiritual bondage that may have been brought into our lives by our ancestors' past actions. As parents, we must then look for these weaknesses in our children and pray for them. This is crucial because the forces of wickedness and evil keeps an inventory of what worked with our past family members and use these same strategies on us based on how successful they were before.

Remember this though, that our heavenly father, who controls all of creation, has the final say in what he allows in, or blocks from, our lives. Remember also that he looks at the heart to determine our experiences. So above all that we do, we must look to him to find out what he is working on in our souls. Finally, we need to daily ask him to govern our thoughts and our emotions so that we can think and act as Jesus did.

As I said before, I ran from the call to write this book up until 2010. But looking back into my childhood and in the years of my adult life, I now see that all along God knew that I was going to write this book, and was preparing me with the experiences that would enable me to write with knowledge, wisdom and understanding. As I put these words together, the memories of my past were awakened, and I saw God's perfect preparation of me. In many experiences in High School and College, I asked, "Why am I doing this? What could I possibly use this for?" There were times when I had conflicts with people and I asked, "Why is this happening to me?" Now I know the purpose of those experiences. Many events that I thought I hid from my memory resurfaced all of a sudden, giving me the necessary tools to write. We are to be very careful how we perceive the experiences that come into our lives. As the Word tells us, we are to trust God with all of our heart and lean not unto our own understanding. We have the promise that if we seek his will in all of our ways, he WILL direct our paths (Proverbs 3:5-6). Only the one who calls us forth into life knows all that there is to know about us. Who then is better to trust?

Experiences can come in the form of 'closed doors'. Maybe God wants you to be strong before he gives you the desire of your heart. Sometimes these closed doors will mean that he wants you to take another direction. If this is the case, he will always provide the way out and an open door to get you to the next destination. Before making any decision, pray and ask what it is that he wants you to do next. Do not make a move until he gives you an answer. While you wait, fill your thoughts with his Word. Be patient, and when God speaks to you, wait again for confirmation. Then with your sure confirmation- obey!

Make a list of some experiences that seemed like closed doors.

How have these experiences affected your life?

Think of the difficult experiences that you are having now. Ask God to show you how these experiences can make you a better person. Write down what he reveals to you.

Thirty Nine

THE CALL- PART SEVEN

"For what shall it profit a man, if he shall gain the whole world, and lose his own soul?"

— (MARK 8:36)

The above passage of scripture asks a very simple question, and this chapter will follow with a very simple answer. It makes no sense spending our entire lives seeking only wealth and fame when all it has ever been about is our souls. God has great wealth already prepared for us, and we will one day live in eternal bliss and glory with him. When our bodies die, all of our riches and fame will not be able to move on with our souls. The only asset that moves from the physical realm of Earth is the soul. That is why we are told that the soul is our greatest asset and that we must protect it at all cost.

Each soul is a uniquely individualized image of God. Why then should we lose the one thing that matters? We MUST keep our own souls. How can we do this? We can keep our own souls by putting on the whole armor of God, which he has given to us as our only source of protection. What is the whole armor? As said

earlier, the armor of God can be simplified by walking in the prin-
ciples of his Spirit, and following the way of Jesus Christ. As also
stated before, it is useless to focus on Jesus' physical appearance.
Rather, we must put our faith in the God who Jesus believed in,
whose power moved him to live, to be sacrificed, then to be res-
urrected. If you want to keep your own soul protected from the
forces of unrighteousness who are determined to destroy it, keep
your armor on and follow the way of Jesus Christ. Know what he
taught. Worship as he worshipped. Believe as he believed. And
love as he loved. Finally, use the sword, which is the Word of God,
and fight as Jesus fought.

What can you do today to be more like Jesus?

Forty

SETTING GOALS

"Shew me thy ways, O LORD; teach me thy paths. Lead
me in thy truth, and teach me: for thou art the God
of my salvation; on thee do I wait all the day"
— (Psalm 25:4-5).

S etting goals can be a successful way of living for God. But
as you were told many times in this book, put him first in
every plan that you make. When our thoughts, emotions and will
are in unison with the Most High's plans, there is so much that we
can look forward to. So as we set goals, let us remember that every-
thing we have is a gift from God and for his purpose. We must be
grounded in this truth that he is sovereign before even thinking to
make plans for our lives. If not, we will be making these plans in
vain. The Word of God tells us,

"Except the LORD build the house, they labour in vain that
build it: except the LORD keep the city, the watchman waketh but
in vain" (Psalm 127:1). Our knowledge of who he is, and what his
law says, should be the foundation from which we begin to plan
our lives, whether it be to get married, follow a career path, make

a decision about where to live, or how to raise children. We must make quality time to speak to God and spend time listening to the directions that he gives. We learned that prayer is a two-way street where we not only speak, but also listen to the Most High God. He speaks through his Word, his messengers, and through our dreams and visions. But in order to hear him, we must slow down and take the time to listen.

The journey of life should be travelled with careful planning. Instead of telling God what we want, we must ask him what it is that he wants. When we ask him, he will put the desires in our hearts that will give us results that are for our best interests. My long term goals are: to live a long and healthy life, to retire young, to be reunited with loved ones and see my heavenly father's face when my body dies, and to see many lives turned to God through the work of this book. I also hope that many families will be reunited as a result of learning the truth presented in these pages. These are some goals that I developed after seeking God's will. But I rest knowing that his will is perfect, and that my outcome will be wonderful whether or not my prayers are answered. So, what are your long term goals?

Naturally we must take time to plan out some simple steps that we need to take in order to meet our long-term goals. These baby steps are our short-term goals. As stated time and again in this work, every step we take should be in the knowledge and application of God's principles of truth. Sometimes we will have a goal, but he will tell us "no" or "wait". If we have a bad attitude when he tells us this, it will show that our will has not been totally turned over to him. In that case we must stop, repent, and ask him to help us humbly surrender to his will. And when God tells us to move, or gives us other directions to take, the advice will always line up with his principles of truth.

To test if you have an inspiration from God, always check to make sure that it lines up with the Word. He has shown over and over again that anything other than a harmonious law would be chaos. Our creator is not an author of confusion (1 Corinthians 14:33). There is no shadow of turning with him (James 1:17). He is the same yesterday, today and forever (Hebrews 13:8). And his truth endureth forever (Psalm 100:5). As you ask God to help you plan your short term goals, remember that material things will only last for a short time in this life. We must therefore seek out those things that will help our souls to grow.

In everything you ask God for, sincerely seek his will first for your life. He will give you the desires of your heart because those desires will fit into his divine order. When you do this, you will find that there is less conflict in your life, and everything will flow in harmony. The right people will show up on the scene to provide something that you have just asked for. When you have questions, the answers to them will come quickly. And you will be at peace no matter what happens around you. These are some signs that will let you know that you have surrendered your will totally to God's will. You will not be able to keep up with the many miracles that will happen in your life from day to day. In the book of James it is written:

> From whence come wars and fightings among you? come they not hence, even of your lusts that war in your members? Ye lust, and have not: ye kill, and desire to have, and cannot obtain: ye fight and war, yet ye have not, because ye ask not. Ye ask, and receive not, because ye ask amiss, that ye may consume it upon your lusts (James 4:1-3).

Pay close attention to the passage of scripture above. Be careful what your motives are when asking God for things. When you are not in his will for your life it will be marked by constant conflict and confusion. And no matter what you achieve, you will continue to feel fearful and in need. Remember, focus on surrendering your all to Almighty God and he will make a way where there seems to be no way.

Ask God to take full control of your life and reveal his goals for you before you attempt to answer the following questions.

What are your long term goals?

What are your short term goals?

Conclusion

"I have fought a good fight, I have finished my course, I have kept the faith: Henceforth there is laid up for me a crown of righteousness, which the Lord, the righteous judge, shall give me at that day: and not to me only, but unto all them also that love his appearing"
— (2 Timothy 4:7-8).

Without God we are nothing! It is because he breathed his breath of life into us and made us living souls that we are here today. We were created by him for his purpose alone, and not for our own. It does not matter what we think or what we think we know; the truth remains that we were created by him and for him. Our heavenly father knows everything about us. He knows our hearts and our abilities. He even knew the names that our parents would choose for us even before we were born.

God can do anything he wants to do. But he is not a chaotic creator. He has put everything in order by his perfect law, the foundational principles of truth. These principles were given to all of creation from the beginning of time. Since Adam and Eve disobeyed him, and entered into the knowledge of good and evil, we became mortals. But even though we fell spiritually, God prepared a way for us to be reunited with him once again.

We still have some of his immortal traits within us, one of them being our free-will. God desires that we use our free-will to love and obey him. We show our love and obedience when we are humble, thankful, and faithful in spite of the challenges of our fallen state. When we do this, we put on his whole armor and truly live in his Spirit and in truth.

Our heavenly father has great things planned for us in eternity. Our life on Earth is just a page out of what he has in store for us. Our time here is like a school where we each learn lessons and take a combination of tests. The objective of these tests is to teach us how to love like God loves and how live in total obedience to him. Whether or not we choose to obey, he is sovereign, and will allow any conflict into our lives which will fulfill his divine order and perfect our growth.

Imagine returning home one day to find all of your family members dead! You try to wrap your mind around what is in front of you, while your community mourns your loss. As you make the necessary emergency calls, you receive a call from your doctor, who tells you that you have contacted a disease that is incurable. All of your friends abandon you, except a few, who tell you that these things are happening to you because you are somehow living in sin. You don't believe them because you know that you fear God and try hard to keep his commandments.

This may not be your life, but know that this kind of terror happens to people all over the world each day. Similar things happened to a man named Job in the Bible. When a debilitating illness, the death of loved ones, or some other traumatic event hit us like it did Job, many of us lose hope and desire death. If something like this happens to you will you curse God and live in hopelessness till you die? Or will you continue to be an example of faith, refusing to curse God no matter the intensity of your pain? I hope that you and I both will have the faith and stamina of Job. He proved his faith as he realized that all is God's and he can do whatever he wants to do with the things that he gives us. At that point of spiritual maturity, God redeemed Job's health and allowed him to have another family, blessing him with even more assets than he had before. As we encounter tribulations while here on Earth, let us keep our focus on the life that we are promised in eternity! Our minds must be fixed on obeying God instead of thinking about the *good and evil* of our existence. Let us fight the good fight, stay the course of righteousness, never lose our faith, and finish well!

Stop trying to hide from the mastermind of all creation. Instead, come before his throne in humility. Repent and ask him to reveal his will for your life! Don't wait for your selfish thoughts and ambitions to lead you to destruction. Remember that serving God is not a religion, but a way of life in which we must each strive to live each moment in perfect harmony with him. Know that when you are using your gifts to serve others, you are actually serving him, because all is his. Finally, know that when you dedicate your life to serving God, people may not realize your efforts, and may condemn you because you do not fit the profile that they've created in their minds for you. Realize that living for God does not make you immune from trouble, for it is in our struggles that we learn to focus on him.

He wants each of us to be a perfect soldier, who is unbound by sin, unhindered by anxiety, and free from the chains of spiritual bondage. When you aim to be these things, you take up your rightful place as an Unchained Child of the Most High God. It is his will that you safely escape, and eventually conquer, all battles of life. He has provided the perfect set of tools to keep our souls protected from the forces of wickedness, but we each must decide whether or not we will put on the whole armor of God. If we are to find safety, success and deliverance, we must be clothed in the Spirit, following the example of Jesus Christ each and every day of our lives.

The attacks of the enemy are effective, but God is always in control. Our struggles are real, but we can live the abundant life that Jesus came to reveal. Our creator wants us to have righteousness, peace, and joy in his Spirit regardless of what life brings. The next time you are in a crisis, you can waste your strength trying to do battle by yourself. Or you can lay back in defeat and be crushed by that thing. But if you want to survive, stand confidently in the whole armor of God, and let him reclaim your soul's victory!

About the Author

Author Gillian Herman-Davis is married and the mother of four children. She is formally trained in the fields of International Studies and Childhood Education. She homeschools her children and mentors teenagers. Herman-Davis also uses her life's skills to empower women to succeed in spite of personal challenges, and organizes events to bring communities together. She wrote *Unchained Child of the Most High God* after hitting bottom, repenting and rededicating her life back to God.

Made in the USA
Columbia, SC
30 April 2018